EMILY DICKINSON IN TIME

EMILY DICKINSON IN TIME

Experience and Its Analysis in Progressive Verbal Form

Morag Harris

Foreword by
Meg Harris Wiliams

The Clunie Press

London
KARNAC BOOKS

First published in 1999 by
H. Karnac (Books) Ltd.
58 Gloucester Road
London SW7 4QY

British Library Cataloguing in Publication Data

A C.I.P. record for this book is available from the British Library

ISBN 1 85575 185 2

10 9 8 7 6 5 4 3 2 1

Edited, designed, and produced by Communication Crafts

Printed in Great Britain by BPC Wheatons Ltd, Exeter

for Emily Dickinson
"holy chamber, wrestler and wrestled for"
for giving us all a chance

To my sister Meg, artist and writer, who, at some cardinal points, has also been a friend;

to my husband and children, for putting up with me;

to my entire family of origin and upbringing, for the years of intense happiness and unhappiness we had together, whose preciousness I have learnt to bear a little better than I once was able;

to Diana, to Luisa, and to Margot, for continuing it, with unstinting kindness and patience;

to my friends Lilla Crisafulli, Gabriella Morisco, and Massimo Bacigalupo; and to the other teachers and scholars whose work, and company, has shown me, indeed, that "Love, like literature, is 'its exceeding great reward'"

I dedicate the effort put into this.

[the quotations are from Dickinson's Letters 210 and 410, respectively]

CONTENTS

FOREWORD

Meg Harris Williams

Emily Dickinson presents a uniquely enigmatic face to literary scholarship, not just because of her idiosyncratic character as an individual and as a poet, but because her entire corpus of c. 1,775 poems, some of which she left tied up in little packages (like the Brontë sisters), is, unlike the Brontës', undated. Anyone attempting to study her work systematically cannot but be impressed by the effectiveness of her revenge on the literary establishment. All consideration of her development as a poet, and hence of the meaningfulness of her poetic activity, is hampered if not crippled by this uncertainty of chronological sequence. Hypothetical approximate datings have been made on the basis of handwriting and biographical events, assuming that she made fair copies at about the time of composition; but inevitably these depend on conjectures about her practice and about the correlation between internal and external events, which cannot be confirmed without greater knowledge of her growth as a poet—hence leading us in a vicious circle. The fact is that without any trustworthy chronological sequence founded on the evolution of her own use of poetic language, our observation of her development, and ultimately of her identity as a poet, remains tenuous. Most studies of Emily Dickinson's poetic practice concentrate on making thematic and typological links between the poems. Morag Harris's approach, however, is unique in focusing on the problem of poetic development by means of its essential factor—poetic language. She has been enabled to do this by making particular use of some of the key letters from Emily Dickinson's extraordinary legacy of c. 1,000 letters, some of which are dated or dateable from their discursive content and hence provide a rich chronological record of what Emily Dickinson termed her "wrestling" (Poem 201; Letter 967) with words—those "numerals of Eden": words in the process of being pressed into metaphor. Far more than even the letters of Keats (which they most nearly resemble), these read as poems-in-the-making.

Harris shows how the kind of experimentation with language and the kind of relationships with external figures and events represented in them are very much on the borderline of poetic internal drama, and as Dickinson's technique progresses some letters become exclusively internal or mental action, as in poetry itself. On these letters, therefore, she bases her own account of Dickinson's developing relationship with the poetic spirit, to which poetic language is—more than mere technique—the key. Although Harris regards her account as only a pilot study owing to its limited scope, her approach demonstrates a new foundation for our access to Dickinson's evolving idea of poetry, which could lead eventually to a more significant dating of her poems in line with the language of the letters, in so far as these both express that elusive phenomenon "poetic language", which always needs to be distinguished from the everyday use of language for communicating information. The "numerals of Eden" belong to a golden not a brazen world (in Sidney's famous distinction); they are not signs to be understood automatically, but symbols to be read with spiritual searching—to be illuminated as they illuminate.

A dating of the poems based on these means will always remain—scientifically speaking—speculative and conjectural rather than deductively proven. But, then, poets have always insisted that a little imagination and vision is necessary to read poems as well as to write them; and it would be characteristic of Emily Dickinson to try to withdraw herself from the kind of intrusive scrutiny she abhorred and to invent a sort of quest or pilgrimage for the reader which (she might hope) *could* not involve plucking out the heart of her mystery as a poet. As it happens, one feels there was something cruel and tantalizing in the manner of her legacy, which has, if anything, damaged her reputation through her inaccessibility: many scholars, baffled by her sphinx-like rebuffal, have concluded that her thought underwent no real or consistent development, and that correspondingly her language is "fanciful" rather than "imaginative" (in the Coleridgean sense): a sophisticated game using self-referential qualities ("fixities and definites", as Coleridge would say), rather than "dissolving to recreate". Thus, Emily Dickinson has become easy prey for the mechanical and behaviourist type of linguistic criticism that recurrently comes into fashion. The absence of firm ground for observation, in the form of chronological sequence, is more likely to result in a judgement of a "fragmentary" opus that expresses no overall view of life than in imaginative intimacy. Undaunted by this, Harris takes Dickinson's ambiguous and shrewd command in one of her letters: "Make lamplighter of me" as a challenge—not to 'burn' the letters but, instead, to use them as a guide to the burning centre of her poetic language. She begins with the conviction that the poetic diction of the poems was elaborated equally and reciprocally in the letters, in a form of fascinating interweaving in which the primary onus of poetically charged language could shift instantaneously from prose to verse. Language conflicts rehearsed in one form might find fulfilment in the other, not vice versa; indeed, sometimes it is the prose language of a letter that is really poetic in this essential sense, while the language of a verse that may be enclosed with the letter on the same theme may be more simple or banal. Thus at times the true poetic energy of her "wrestling on the spar" could be channelled into her un-ordinary prose in a way that, as Harris suggests, perhaps gave greater license to chaos than her stringent verse style could ever have permitted. So there is a sense in which the writing of the letters seems to have been emotionally necessary to the creation of the poems as finished products. Harris describes how, immersed in the language of these letters, the reader is overwhelmed by the density of language and association, unable to see the wood for the trees. Inevitably, something of this quality filters through into our experience of her own account of Dickinson's enigmatic expression, which has to be examined microscopically for the true quality of its poetic language to be determined; indeed, the main focus of the book is on only three letters, chronologically and developmentally distinct. And in retrospect, as Harris shows, a clear line of development emerges, which strongly illustrates the inseparability of thought and technique in Dickinson's poetic language, and the evolution of a particular poetic identity—"schooled", as Keats would say, to "make it a soul".

There is, of course, a difference between looking for an overall 'view of life' in a poet's work and following the evolution of mental or spiritual process that results in an aesthetic object or art-symbol. In a sense the entire body of an author's work comprises an aesthetic object—the expression of a correspondence with psychic reality that is itself not static but evolutionary. It is the latter, rather than the cataloguing of explicit philosophical positions, that is the author's concern in this book. And this is appropriate to Emily Dickinson's own view of her search for "the Chiefest words", not as fixities and definites, but as a "chest to put the Alive in". Emily Dickinson's most fervent period of creativity has generally been assumed to be the period that would appear to be the time of her greatest productivity (around the years 1858–1865). But the approach to studying the processes of poetic language made by Morag Harris in this book suggests, on the contrary, that the *quality* of her language—in its compression and capacity for meaningfulness—intensified over the years in a clear progression. If this is so in the letters, whose chronology is known, then it should be so in the poems, though their chronology is not: for her overall ability to use language becomes more poetic. Linguistic research into creativity and mental processes—into the operation of what has been called "deep grammar" and symbol-formation—is still in its infancy, and there is a perennial temptation to sink back into simplistic explanations based on language as a sign-system for communication, since this aspect of language is easier to analyse than the expressive function of symbol creation. The following study, however, firmly takes the bull by the horns in a way that makes a lasting contribution to our observation of creative language processes and of how the creative creates itself.

Meg Harris Williams

PREFACE

This volume is the correlation of nearly twenty years' exercise and concern with language, whose principal point of departure and return—or "dancing and departure", as Henry Reed might have called it—has been, and perhaps will always be, the life-work of the poet concerned. Nothing more.

The ramification of this concern into the limited concrete viewing points that constitute this present shape has taken place within the vast and particular horizon of Susanne K. Langer's enquiry into what it is in human experience that may be captured in language, the nature of those forms of language that capture such experience, and their interrelation; into how this process of relationship may be generated, received, and propagated, both in the individual and in social being in its widest sense.

EMILY DICKINSON IN TIME

Language, in its literal capacity, is a stiff and conventional medium, unadapted to the expression of genuinely new ideas, which usually have to break in upon the mind through some great bewildering metaphor. . . . [But] Ideas first adumbrated in fantastic form become real intellectual property only when discursive language rises to their expression. . . . (p. 201)

Artistic symbols . . . are untranslatable . . . This is true even of poetry, for though the material of poetry is verbal, its import is not the literal assertion made in the words, but *the way the assertion is made*. . . . (p. 260)

"Artistic truth", so called, is the truth of a symbol to the forms of feeling—nameless forms, but recognisable when they appear in sensuous replica. . . . To understand the "idea" in a work of art is therefore more like having a new experience than like entertaining a new proposition. . . . (p. 263)

Susanne K. Langer, *Philosophy in a New Key*

I

Emily Dickinson's estate and her inheritors: perfection and confusion

1. Her sanity

William Luce describes in the Preface to his play, *The Belle of Amherst*,[1] how:

> it was my hope to depict the humanity and reasonableness of Emily Dickinson's life. . . . The strange faces of genius are enigmatic to the structured mind, probing for final answers. Causation seems as elusive as "melody or witchcraft" [Letter 261]. . . .[2]
>
> The essential Emily of my play is secretly saying to the audience, "Pardon my sanity." [L185] Pardon my jubilation in

---

[1] Boston, Houghton Mifflin, 1978. The play itself has inevitably become the object of critical attention: see, for example, Maravene Loeschke's "Challenges of Portraying Emily Dickinson's in William Luce's Play 'The Belle of Amherst'", in the *Emily Dickinson Journal*, Niwot, CO (1993), 2:2, 124–129.

[2] All references to Dickinson's letters (L) and prose fragments (PF) are taken from *The Letters of Emily Dickinson*, eds. Johnson and Ward, Cambridge, MA: the Belknap Press of Harvard University Press, 1958.

> Nature, my terror of midnight, my childlike wonder at love, my white renunciation. . . .
>
> I read and re-read the . . . biographical studies, . . . her letters, . . . her poems. . . . Gradually, Emily's story emerged, as if she were telling it herself.
>
> My colleagues . . . also pored over the Dickinson material. . . . We all seemed joined together in love in this enterprise of simple beauty. . . .
>
> *The Belle of Amherst* is a love affair with language, a celebration of all that is beautiful and poignant in life. As it turns out, shy Miss Emily was writing for theater as surely as she breathed. In her every evocative phrase there is theatrical texture. On stage, the strange ways of Emily Dickinson become dramatic qualities in an arena large enough to give them the look of "divinest Sense" [Poem 435]. . . .[3]

To Luce's list could be added 'my occasional submission, my sense of humiliation, my jealousy, my despair, my rage at injustice, my desire for vengeance, my biting scepticism, my pugnacity', and many other of the rich range of feelings through which Dickinson takes us. Whether or not one considers Luce's play as historically accurate, certainly I think the spirit he evoked of the poet is true, and that his play is what she longed for: a genuine, articulate response to her poetic work, a 'poem' responding to a 'poem', fulfilment of "the ruling power and purpose of art", in Langer's terms.[4]

Emily Dickinson called our life "checkered",[5] and there is nothing automatic or simple about this process of artistic growth and response. What did Dickinson's "sanity" involve, in what did it consist, how was it built and sustained? Against what obstacles did it have to pit itself, and were these internal or external or both? How did Emily Dickinson become a poet, how did her use of the

---

[3] All references to the poems (P) are taken from the 3-volume *Poems of Emily Dickinson including variant readings*, ed. T. H. Johnson, Cambridge, MA: the Belknap Press of Harvard University Press [1951] 1955.

[4] See *Feeling and Form: A Theory of Art*, London: Routledge and Kegan Paul [1953] 1970, 67 (henceforth: Langer, *Feeling*).

[5] L108; also reported in Jay Leyda, *The Years and Hours of Emily Dickinson*, New Haven, CT: Yale University Press, I, 264 (henceforth *Leyda*).

symbolic form of poetic language, the lighting of that lamp's wick (P883),[6] develop to become that inhering vital Light, which, the more it is looked upon, both "widens its breadth" and "becomes more widespread", illuminates more aspects as it becomes more widely visible itself, like the disseminating of suns' circumference?[7] How did her language develop to become those forms that are such a source of vitality to us today?

2. The problem of knowing what she wrote

We know with some certainty now the exasperatingly tortuous story of the publication of Dickinson's manuscripts, although we know vastly less, and to a vastly lesser degree of certainty, of the development of these. I will try to recount this as briefly and faithfully as possible, and against this background, try to show the reasons for my proposal for a method of research into her work.

We know that before 1858 Dickinson had started writing poems; we know that eleven of these were published in her lifetime, six of which (nos. 3, 35, 214, 216 [1859 version], 228, 986) appeared in the *Springfield Republican*, a magazine edited by a family friend,

---

[6] The Poets light but Lamps—
Themselves—go out—
The Wicks they stimulate—
If vital Light

Inhere as do the Suns—Each Age a Lens
Disseminating their
Circumference—

[7] Cf. Coleridge: "Christ ... is not described primarily and characteristically as a Teacher, but as a *Doer*—a Light indeed, but an effective Light, a Light of the Sun causing what it shews, as well as shewing what it *causes*—", *The Notebooks of Samuel Taylor Coleridge*, 3 vols, ed. Kathleen Coburn, London: Routledge and Kegan Paul, 1973, III, 3581 (henceforth Coleridge, *Notebooks*).

Samuel Bowles.[8] We know these poems were edited, probably to her regret, to conform to the dullness of circumscribed contemporary taste. We know she engaged in years of correspondence with Bowles, talking obliquely about her poetry and her person. We know that, disappointed in his attitude to the unique form of her verse, and after the publication of the first three of the above, she wrote to Thomas Wentworth Higginson in 1862 after reading his article, "Ought Women Learn the Alphabet?" in the February 1859 issue of the *Atlantic Monthly*,[9] and then his "Letter to a Young Contributor" in the April 1862 issue of the same, hoping to be better understood as a poet. We know she corresponded with him for the rest of her life, enclosing overall 6 or 7 poems in that Spring 1862 (216 [1861 version],[10] 319, 320, 318; 322, 321, 86 probably), responding to his advice and admonishments in his article in her own partially highly ironic, but partially sincerely pleading and enquiring way. She wanted a real interlocutor, and in part saw the potential for one in him. We know Higginson felt she was extraordinary but did not know what to make of her. "All men say 'What' to me", she observed (L271).

We may believe, following Ruth Miller's brilliant, laborious, and strangely little-quoted reconstruction of Dickinson's life as a writer in relation to the context of language around her,[11] that Bowles', and then Higginson's, failure to understand her, partly as a writer and, in the former case, also as a woman, caused such a storm of agonizing disappointment and rage and despair in her, especially since she saw that this was not the lot of other more

---

[8] The other five poems were published in New York in 1864, according to Karen Dandurand's findings: "New Dickinson Civil War Publications", *American Literature* (March 1984), 56, 1, 17–27. See also her earlier "Another Dickinson Poem Published in Her Lifetime", *American Literature*, Durham, NC (1982 Oct), 54, 3, 434–437.

[9] See Cynthia Griffin Wolff, *Emily Dickinson*, Radcliffe Biography Series, Reading, MA: Addison-Wesley, 1986, 251.

[10] Johnson, in the Variorum edition (*Poems*, p. xxvi) claimed that the *Springfield Republican* version and the version sent to Higginson were the same. But see Ruth Miller's detailed discussion of Dickinson's substitution of the second stanza in the letter (in *The Poetry of Emily Dickinson*, Middletown, CT: Wesleyan University Press, 1968, 45–46; henceforth *Miller*).

[11] Ibid., especially Chapters 3, 4, and 5.

modest women writers around her, that it probably gave her the emotional grounds for the three thousand or so poems and letters that were to make of her undoubtedly one of the greatest poets of all time.

The technically solid biography by R. B. Sewall,[12] however, shows echoes in Dickinson's language of the minister Charles Wadsworth's forcefully poetic sermons, as well as recounting their meetings and few extant but rather haunting letters and comments and enquiries about each other. Luce also obviously assented to this idea of some significant congruence in their mentality and portrays Wadsworth as the "man", the "Master" in Emily Dickinson's mind. However, as we know, such congruence may not necessarily be reflected in historical fact.

The point is not to dig out the supposed "Master's" identity (perhaps there were several, after all),[13] but rather to come to terms with the meaning of the symbolic expression created by the poet from her experience, her conjoined thoughts and feelings; to understand the process by which, from the inevitably external data of experience,[14] her imaginative grasp of feeling, that "idea containing . . . many minute yet closely related parts . . . many relations

---

[12] *The Life of Emily Dickinson*. New York: Farrar, Straus and Giroux, 444–462 henceforth Sewall, *Life*).

[13] See Griffin Wolff, *Emily Dickinson*, 406: "she may have become emotionally involved with some other man whose identity is not known. By the late 1850s, a great many distinguished speakers came regularly to Amherst; . . . At this distance of time, it would be difficult even to name all the men Emily Dickinson might have come to know during these years".

[14] See Langer, *Philosophy*, 248: "all elementary symbolic forms have their origin in something else than symbolic interest"; and Langer, *Feeling*, Part II, Chapter 4: "Semblance", *passim*. For her acknowledged debt to Schiller for her elaboration of this last concept, see his *On the Aesthetic Education of Man in a Series of Letters* (c.1793–95) (eds. Elizabeth M. Wilkinson and L. A. Willoughby, Oxford: Clarendon Press [1967] 1982; henceforth Schiller, *Aesthetic Education*). Dickinson may have had access to some of these, also through parts translated by De Quincey (1824), by Carlyle (whom she admired, or so we may presume from the portrait hanging in her bedroom) (1831, 1869); or to more complete versions, such as that published by George Eliot's friend and colleague, J. Chapman, in 1845, or that of the American translator Charles J. Hempel in 1861, all of which are described in Schiller, *Aesthetic Education*, Appendix II: "Translators and Translation", 338–347; see also notes 56 & 152 below.

within relations" described so beautifully by Langer,[15] became "projected" into symbolic expression, such that it becomes available to us all to "have a new experience", to expand and educate our sentient being, such that it becomes universal.[16]

We know that later in life she was deeply attached to a friend of her father's, Judge Otis Phillips Lord, apparently after the death of his first wife, and that this attachment was reciprocated. Mabel Loomis Todd reports Sue's viperine affirmation that Emily and Lavinia had no sense of "morality" and that Emily was found reclining in "a man's arms" (probably Lord's) one day in the drawing room.[17] One can only hope that the drawing room was not the only place she reclined in his arms.

We do not know with any certainty when or to whom the extraordinary draftlike "Master" letters were written, though we conjecture composition round about 1860.[18] More worksheets, the impressions of volcanic work in progress, than objective, communicative letters, they were a sort of explosive, watershed point in her development of poetic language: she begins to show us her constructing of her self, her personal identity, what Keats called "the genius of Poetry . . . [working] out its own salvation in a man . . . that which is creative . . . [creating] itself".[19] Her identity as poet fused irreversibly with her person, in that firmly projected, psychi-

---

[15] See Langer, *Philosophy in a New Key*, Cambridge, MA: Harvard University Press [1942] 1979 (henceforth: Langer, *Philosophy*), p. 93: "An idea that contains too many minute yet closely related parts, too many relations within relations, cannot be 'projected' into discursive form; it is too subtle for speech".

[16] In this connection, it is interesting to see Richard Holmes' description of Coleridge (*Early Visions*, London: Hodder & Stoughton, 1989, 218n.: henceforth *Holmes*) as he: "organised a personal dictionary of German words under ten generic categories" which show that he approached language "poetically, less a taxonomy of objects, but rather as a creative power in itself, 're-inventing' the world in terms of human perceptions, rather like the Epic poem he was continually urging upon Wordsworth".

[17] Sewall, *Life*, 195.

[18] Two are in ink with corrections in pencil, one in pencil throughout, and Johnson's dating in 1958 conjectured on the basis of handwriting: L187, 1858; L233, 1861; L248, 1862. Previously only extracts from these had been made public, with the date deliberately falsified. The "complete" texts were not made available until 1955. See Sewall, *Life*, 512. It is not publicly known whether or to whom they were ever sent.

[19] Letter to Hessey, 8 October 1818.

cally distanced way we see it in "This was a Poet" (P448). With all her energy she begins to attempt, though she oscillates, to leap from the metaphors of being the dependent "best little girl",[20] to those of the adult couple's side-by-side though separate promenade toward the sunset, as she grows in stature. One is reminded in a different light of her wide network of "letting go" metaphors in verse and prose, often, and in some instances probably mistakenly, read as suicidal.[21] And as I will suggest later, it seems this passage involved her very concrete recognition of the agonizing difficulty of genuine communication between people—where this is attempted at all—of being "known as also you are known",[22] to the extent that, except through her art, at a certain point she gave up trying. Hugh McDiarmid once described this point in his life as "taking the long view".[23] Keats called this achievement "Negative Capability". Ruth Miller's account is worth reporting:

> [Dickinson] disagreed with the judgment of Samuel Bowles; . . . She did make a second effort; she did seek another critical

---

[20] L248: "Master—open your life wide, and take me in forever, I will never be tired—I will never be noisy when you want to be still. I will be [glad] [as the] your best little girl . . . I shall not want any more . . . ".

[21] One thinks, for example, of "After great pain a formal feeling comes" (P341), placed by A. Alvarez at the front of his moving study of suicide, *The Savage God* (Harmondsworth: Penguin, 1971). Still, it seems to me that the more one looks at it, the less evident it is that it is suicidal, and that the "letting go", reached through all the progressive chain of lexical transformations—"formal–ceremonious–tombs–stiff–bore–mechanical–wooden–contentment" into "remembered–outlived–freezing–recollect–Snow–chill–stupor"—is as open to an idea of release and regeneration as of annihilation. One sees the ghost of this metaphor in very many working "images"—holding on–letting go; freeing–imprisoning; subjecting–enabling; killing–inspiring—for example, P664,"Of all the Souls that stand create"; ironically in P861, "Split the Lark—and you'll find the Music". I believe the essential transformation of the basic idea—relinquishment of possession of the object to make space instead for *love* of it, and respect for its freedom—was worked out, realized, both linguistically and emotionally, in the "Master" letters, particularly L233 and L248 (who can tell how many more of these letters there were originally?), much as I have tried to describe it in: "Representations of the Male in the Female Imagination: The Brontës and Dickinson", in *Gramma: Journal of Theory and Criticism* (The Erotic in Women's Poetry) 4 (1996), Thessaloniki, Aristotle University Publications, 129–151.

[22] I *Corinthians*, 13:12. Also see Section II.3.

[23] British TV programme, 1992.

> judgment from a well-known literary man, but T. W. Higginson's opinion was the same. Her defense collapsed and from that time on Emily Dickinson made no further attempt to convince anyone. [p. 188]

It is moving to read Miller's observation (p. 189) that in spite of Dickinson's great disappointment in her relationship with Bowles, there is only one poem on record (1282) in which she denigrates him, as opposed to the many poems frankly wrestling with rage, hurt, and disappointment. There is, however, ample mention throughout her letters of her "box of Phantoms" (L177), and it is never quite clear whether these "phantoms" represent people she has lost or people she has herself kicked out, like that ambiguous "Guest [host/ghost/stranger?] who would be gone" in "As imperceptibly as grief" (1540). As she said herself (L 245):"Odd, that I, who say 'no' so much, cannot bear it from others. Odd, that I, who run from so many, cannot brook that one turn from me". A poem like "He was my host—he was my guest" (1721)—which probably *is* later—shows us the relations between the terms from another vertex.

We know she came to realize the difficulties that she as a poet, and that "great bewildering metaphor", her poetry, would come up against in being recognized, understood and accepted in her own day, when so-called art forms had become "literal and self-imitating";[24] we know she started making fair copies of her poems,

[24] Langer, *Feeling,* 403: "Indifference to art is the most serious sign of decay in any institution; nothing bespeaks its old age more eloquently than that art, under its patronage, becomes literal and self-imitating". [See Willis Buckingham, "Poetry Readers and Reading in the 1890s: Emily Dickinson's First Reception" in ed. James L. Machor, *Readers in History: Nineteenth Century American Literature and the Contexts of Response,* Baltimore, MD: Johns Hopkins University Press, 1993). It is difficult not to recall, in this connection, a comment made by Alice James in her diary (reported in H. Waggoner, "The Transcendent Self", *Criticism: A Quarterly for Literature & the Arts* (1965), Detroit, MI, 297–334: "It is reassuring to hear the English pronouncement that Emily Dickinson is fifth-rate, they have such a capacity for missing quality". (See also Ann Lilliedahl, "Emily Dickinson in Europe: Her Reputation in Selected Countries", Washington, DC: UP of America, 1981.) A brief diachronic overview of critical reception may be useful here: (a) (1890) "It has always seemed to me that it would be unwise to perpetuate Miss Dickinson's poems. They are quite as remarkable for defects as for beauties and

and started grouping these together into threaded booklets, or potential booklets—as if for universal publication, we now assume. We do not know when she began this concrete linking activity. We do not really know whether this was work-in-progress or work she considered completed when she died. These poems and groups-of-poems are all undated.

---

are generally devoid of true poetical qualities" (Letter from Thomas Niles, editor of the Boston publishing house, to Higginson, quoted by Johnson in his Introduction to the Variorum edition, *Poems*, p. xliv. In 1883, curiously, Niles had in vain tried to persuade Dickinson to allow him to publish a volume of her poems; see L813b); (b) (1937): "Whitman and Emily Dickinson . . . drove forward on the élan of their natural aptitudes for language, resorting regardless to whatever props, scaffolds, obsessive symbols or intellectual mechanisms came to hand, but neither of them finding satisfactory form. . . . Neither her personal education nor the habit of her society as she knew it ever gave her the least inkling that poetry is a rational and objective art and most so when the theme is self-expression" (R. P. Blackmur, "Emily Dickinson: Notes on Prejudice and Fact," in *Southern Review*, 3, reprinted in *Language as Gesture: Essays in Poetry*, New York, 1952, and in *The Recognition of Emily Dickinson: Selected Criticism since 1890*, eds. Caesar R. Blake & Carlton F. Wells, Ann Arbor, MI: University of Michigan Press, 1964); (c) (1938): "Her meter, at its worst—that is, most of the time—is a kind of stiff sing-song; her diction, at its worst, is a kind of poetic nursery jargon; and there is a remarkable continuity of manner . . . between her worst and her best poems . . . there is nearly always a margin of ambiguity in our final estimate of even her most extraordinary work [. . .]. Her best poems . . . can never be isolated certainly and defensibly from her defects" (Yvor Winters, "Emily Dickinson and the Limits of Judgement", in *In Defense of Reason*, New York: William Morrow, 1947); (d) (1952): Richard Chase suggested that we only really read her for a group of about 50 out of the 1,775 verse poems that she allowed us to keep (*Emily Dickinson*, London: Methuen); (e) (1963):"My own prediction is that Emily Dickinson will grow stronger with the years as we continue to outdistance the sentimentalities that still cling to her. Her eccentricities will fall into perspective. We will become increasingly aware of the toughness and sinew of her poetry, its challenge to our understanding. We will test our knowledge of humanity against hers and find that we can learn on almost every front. Far from the little figure of frustrations and renunciations and regrets, we will come to see her as a poet of great strength, courage and singleness of purpose" (R. B. Sewall in *A Collection of Critical Essays*, Englewood Cliffs, Prentice-Hall); (f) (1986): "Given the objective social prohibitions Emily Dickinson confronted . . . it would have been an easy thing for the poetry to become contaminated with resentment. One of Dickinson's greatest personal victories is that she did not allow this contamination to take place. She was astute enough to realize how urgently the quality of

3. The problem of not knowing when she wrote it

Naturally, this being the case, at her death, the story became complicated for posterity, to put it mildly. When Dickinson died, aged 56, after the loss of her father, mother, then of her "little Ajax" (L868), her 8-year-old nephew Gilbert; after having refused the insistence of Helen Hunt Jackson that she publish, the "chest" she kept the "Alive" (L233)—her poems—in, it was opened, and the threaded and unthreaded booklets, packets, and loose worksheets were finally "let go" and allowed to "take the chances for Heaven" (except for what may have been destroyed, of course).[25] At Lavinia's bidding, Mabel Loomis Todd, and eventually the recalcitrant Higginson, set to work on making the poems respectable and acceptable for publication. They promptly undid all the fascicles (loose pages were returned to Lavinia Dickinson, thence to Susan Dickinson and her daughter, Martha Dickinson Bianchi), mixing the fair copies up with all the variant and work sheets, numbering them casually. We will never know with certainty the original grouping Dickinson left, although Johnson's successive labours in the 1950s with handwriting, matching pinholes, qualities of paper, and so on have probably restored much accurately.

---

her art depended upon her success in reaching her readers. . . . She was willing to transfer all the energy of living into the creation of poetry—willing to exchange a transient but nonetheless palpable "self" for a disembodied Voice that exists intact and unchanged now, more than a century later [. . .]—a vibrant, often commanding Voice that not only speaks but speaks to you. . . . In sum, she wanted to make the terms of existence that were meaningful to the Voice of her poetry relevant to the terms of existence by which her readers defined their own lives—whoever those readers might be, in no matter what time or place. And the miracle is, she succeeded" (Cynthia Griffin Wolff, *Emily Dickinson*).

[25] Dickinson apparently gave Lavinia instructions to burn correspondence sent to her by other people. She did not, to my knowledge, ask for her correspondence to others—whether sent, or not (like perhaps the "Master" drafts)—to be burned (though much of it has been lost, or simply not found, anyway). Presumably she meant something else by "Make lamplighter of me" (L213, and see reworking of metaphor in P883). See Sewall, *Life*, 96 & 750.

4. The consequent problems in its publication

The *First Series* came out (Boston, MA: Roberts Bros., 1890) and was a rapid, lucrative success. After this, Higginson, more willingly, helped to edit the *Second Series* (1891) which contained some of Dickinson's letters to him, for he had sensitively remarked on the extraordinary power of her prose style. In their affectionate yet timorous enthusiasm and desire to get Dickinson into the world as she deserved, these first editors changed rhymes, the verse form, substituted MS words with their own, selected words from variants according to their own preferences—or anxiety to compromise—without feeling bound by the original form or by the suggestion of overall shape Dickinson seems to have given to at least part of her work in the fascicles, what Ruth Miller will call "long link-poem[s]" (*Miller,* 249). (It seems conjecturable from handwriting, paper, and so on that her fair copy groupings were not dictated by a principle of chronology—she grouped poems from different periods.) At this point, the editors set about preparing publication of an edition of the letters. This publication (1894), however, ended up complicating and mystifying the Dickinson's person more than was already the case, increasing the barrier between the public and the significance of the poetic work, between the public and her *sanity.* With the publication of the letters coming up and the now juicy forecasts regarding sales, the "real life" (L161) issue of recompense reared its ugly head. "Test's severe repairs" to fictions "are permitted all", Dickinson tells us (L330). Well, the Todd–Dickinson relationship did not stand up to it.

Lavinia had made a lot out of the sale of the first two series of poems; Todd and Higginson had been given only 100 dollars between them. Austin tried to get Lavinia to agree to give Todd (now sole editor of the letters) some share in the profit. This evidenced a rift between the two women, and Austin tried to give Todd a piece of Dickinson land bordering on her property instead, but he died suddenly. Lavinia signed the deed bequeathing the land in spite of Austin's death, since Todd was still editing the *Third Series* of poems. But as soon as this was out (1896: by now 499 poems—less than a third of Dickinson's total work—had been published, and in corrupted versions), she took Todd to court to go back on this, and won. Forgivably, Mabel Loomis Todd shut away all her Dickinson MSs and refused to have any more to do with publishing the work. In the years that followed, the Todd–Dickinson quarrel was taken up, in the old way, by Mabel's and by Susan's daughters, with a sort of ping-pong series of publications of bowdlerized poems, fragments, anecdotes, and pure fantasy, whatever remained divided between the two houses, broadly as follows:

1914: *The Single Hound,* ed. Martha Dickinson Bianchi. Poems given by Dickinson to Sue. No fascicle poems, so no variants used;

1918: *The Point of View,* Martha Gilbert Dickinson Bianchi. A form of novel seeming implicitly about the Dickinsons, depicting the eccentricities of a Puritanical New England family and alimenting the 'insane streak' myth;

1924: *The Life and Letters of Emily Dickinson*: ed. M. Dickinson Bianchi. In the shape of a love story, with Wadsworth now suggested as the loved man;

1924: *The Complete Poems of Emily Dickinson* ed. M. Dickinson Bianchi (now sole copyright holder). A conglomeration of the *First, Second,* and *Third Series* of *Poems* and her own *The Single Hound.* All textual emendations of first printings retained;

1929: *Further Poems.* ed. Martha Dickinson Bianchi. Full of errors, leading some reviewers to question the authenticity of many poems;

1931: more *Letters,* ed. Mabel Loomis Todd. Those formerly suppressed or expurgated, including Clark brothers' (referring to Wadsworth) published, with a few poems added haphazardly;

1932: *Emily Dickinson: Face to Face,* ed. M. Dickinson Bianchi. Corrupted versions, letters, scraps of prose, anecdotes, Sue's formerly erased name restored;

1935: *Unpublished Poems of Emily Dickinson,* eds. M. Dickinson Bianchi and Alfred Leete Hampson;

1945: *Bolts of Melody*, eds. Millicent Todd Bingham and Mabel Loomis Todd, who died during the book's preparation. All documents in their possession by now published.

This last publication represented the success of Millicent Todd Bingham in getting her mother to take up Emily Dickinson's work again and to show how inaccurate, bowdlerized, and incomplete Martha Dickinson Bianchi's versions of the poems were. Eventually, in 1950, the whole estate was transferred to Harvard University, and the then heroic labour of global re-editing was taken on by Thomas H. Johnson.[26] The manuscripts were delivered

[26] At this distance of time, however, see William H. Matchett's letter to the *Times Literary Supplement*, 2 July 1982, regarding the often, perhaps typically, sad consequences with time of the "institutionalized" monumentalization of creative work, where the "guardian-of-the-faith" attitude ends up—in the face of everything the artist ever begged for—in fact imposing a barrier, instead of opening a door, between such work and its intended recipients and heirs. However, see in this connection Jo Anne Cappeluti, "Fading Ratios: Johnson's Variorum Edition of Emily Dickinson's Poetry", in the *Emily Dickinson Journal*, 1992, Niwot CO., 1:2, 100–120. And since the informing principle of this study was conceived and its method first constructed, studies that have contemplated the aesthetic significance of the prose–poetry relationship in Dickinson's work have proliferated, and include those by: Suzanne Juhasz (Reading Emily Dickinson's Letters", in *ESQ: A Journal of the American Renaissance*, 1984 3rd Quart., Pullman WA., 30:3, 170–192); Sharon M. Harris "The 'Cloth of Dreams': Dream Imagery in Dickinson's Poetry and Prose", in *Dickinson Studies*, 1988, 68, 3–16; Sarah Wider ("Corresponding Worlds: The Art of Emily Dickinson's Letters", in the *Emily Dickinson Journal*, 1992, 1:1, 39–53); Agnieszka Salska ("Emily Dickinson's Letters: The Making of a Poetics", in ed. J. Maszewska, *Crossing Borders: American Literature and Other Artistic Media*, Lodz, Peoria IL, Polish Scientific, Spoon River, 1992); William M. Decker ('A Letter Always Seemed to Me Like Immortality': The Correspondence of Emily Dickinson" in *ESQ: A Journal of the American Renaissance*, 1993, Pullman WA, 39:2–3, 77–105); S. Jaret McKinstry ("'How Lovely Are the Wiles of Words!—or, 'subjects Hinder Talk': The Letters of Emily Dickinson" in eds. and introds. T. F. Berg, A. S. Elfenebin, J. Larsen, E. K. Sparks, and fwd., S. Gilbert, *Engendering the Word: Feminist Essays in Psychosexual Poetics*, Urbana, IL: University of Illinois Press, 1989); R. N. Graves ("Dickinson's Letters 263 and 271", in *Explicator*, Spring 1995, Washington DC, 53:3, 152–156); E. L. Hart ("The Elizabeth Whitney Putnam Manuscripts and New Strategies for Editing Emily Dickinson's Letters", in the *Emily Dickinson Journal*, 1995, Niwot CO., 4:1, 44–74); R. G. Lambert (*A Critical Study of Emily Dickinson's Letters: The Prose of a Poet*, USA, Edwin Mellen Press, 1996). Other studies that work with an idea

piecemeal, with Todd's original spurious numbering on them. Johnson attempted to put poems in chronological order on the basis of external evidence—watermarks, handwriting, folds in paper, and so on, and in 1955 the 3-volume Variorum edition of the poems came out, followed by the 3-volume edition of the letters in 1958.

5. The issue of her motives for not telling us when she wrote it

At this stage in history, now that the work is available in somewhat more complete and less distorted shape than before, and our discursive analyses may help us to begin to make "real intellectual property" of the "genuinely new idea, ... first adumbrated ... through [Dickinson's] great bewildering metaphor", it is easy to belittle these first editors and relatives in the face of such an uncivil tangle. However, from another point of view, it is difficult not to feel, with M. H. Williams, that:

> there was something cruel and tantalising in the manner of her legacy which has if anything damaged her reputation through her inaccessibility: many scholars, baffled by her sphinx-like rebuffal, have concluded that her thought underwent no real or consistent development, and that correspondingly her language is "fanciful" rather than "imaginative" (in the Coleridgean sense): a sophisticated game using self-referential qualities ("fixities and definites" as Coleridge would say) rather than "dissolving to recreate"....

---

of progressive development in her work include Carol L. Cook ("The Psychic Development of a Woman Writer", in the *University of Dayton Review*, Winter 1987–1988, Dayton OH, 19:1, 111–119); Timothy Morris ("The Development of Dickinson's Style", in *American Literature*, March 1988, Durham NC, 60:1, 26–41).

Indeed, it seems to entail a serious mistake in method to assume that we can be sure that Dickinson regarded these threaded or potentially threaded booklets as absolutely definitive, and not as merely one possible version.[27] Sometimes duplicates seem to have been made of the same poem and placed in different packets (Johnson attributes this to Dickinson's "forgetfulness",[28] incredible in a poet so refined and meticulous as she), just as they were often incorporated into the often dated letters (after all, a form of publication). And this perhaps in a similarly experimental, multifaceted way to Blake's dissolving and reconstituting the order of the *Songs*, experimentally termed "moveability" by Gerda Norvig.[29] Sometimes there are standing marginal variants in poems, sometimes fair copy variant poems,[30] and so on. Furthermore, it seems significant to me that if Dickinson did regard the grouping of these packets and fascicles as ultimately definitive, unmoveable, she never published them as such, nor apparently informed Lavinia or Austin or Mabel Loomis Todd or Helen Hunt Jackson, or any of those who surely loved her, of their formed existence, nor in any case left them with unequivocal indications to posterity.

---

[27] Cf. also Sewall's doubt, *Life*, 538n. Though they do not affect the underlying point made above, other studies hypothesizing the significance of conjectured form in the so-called fascicles include those successively made by Martha L. O'Keefe ("This Edifice: Studies in the Structure of the (13) Fascicles of the poetry of Emily Dickinson", in *Dickinson Studies*, Washington DC (June 1982), 42, 3–15); Diane G. Scholl (Emily Dickinson's Conversion Narratives: A Study of the Fascicles", in *Studies in Puritan American Spirituality*, Lewiston NY (1990), 1, 170–201); Eleanor E. Heginbotham ("Dwelling in Possibilities: The Fascicles of Emily Dickinson", in *Dissertation Abstracts International*, Ann Arbor, MI (July 1993), 54, 1); John Gerlach ("Reading Dickinson: Bolts, Hounds, the Variorum, and Fascicle 39" in the *Emily Dickinson Journal* (1994), 3, 2, 78–99); Dorothy R. Oberhaus (*Emily Dickinson's Fascicles: Method & Meaning*, University Park, PA: Pennsylvania State University Press, 1995).

[28] See Johnson, *Poems*, III, Appendix 7, 1205.

[29] University of Colorado in Boulder: lecture given at Bologna University, Spring 1994.

[30] *Miller*, 250.

6. The later consequences of her not telling us when she wrote it

In her eloquent study, Miller's main bone of contention is the undoing of the fascicles as Dickinson left them, which she affirms distorted our view of the meaning of Dickinson's poetry unnecessarily for many years and encouraged totally fanciful, so misleading, speculation about the poet's life and person. Her description in "The Fascicles" chapter, of Dickinson's supposed groupings of her work overall as a "structured series of poems, the rendering of a conflict in stages of perplexity moving from query to response, to new inquiry to another reply" (p. 270), is very persuasive.[31] Earlier, in a more general chapter "The Poetic Manner", she writes:

> (RE: THEMATIC ANALYSIS)
>
> [pp. 195–198] the poet operated freely within a conglomerate of interchangeable personae and meanings. One poem did not cancel another; taken together the poems extended the scope of her awareness. They enriched one another. . . . The poet may be a woman given to tears, a bard whose mission is the proclamation of the truth, or a mortal, subject to decay. What flies from the grasp of the persona may be a crumb, a ducat, leaves, light, lover, editor, fame, revelation, release; but always there is a pattern in the rendering of Emily Dickinson's subject matter: flight and return. This is the pattern into which she fits all experience. Always there is a presence, a loss, then the assurance of some ultimate re-encounter, some ultimate union. . . . Many of the poems written before 1860 described death as a sad withdrawal into another realm. . . . After 1860–61 the occasion of death is concrete: it is the death of the poet. It is not the meaning of death as a phenomenon, but the experience of spiritual annihilation rendered in physical terms. The religious poems change from theoretic affirmation to renderings of Heaven. The place is populated with angels and martyrs and Jesus, and the poet arrives there in poem after poem, bringing with her the burden of suffering and anguish

[31] But again see Sewall's doubts: *Life*, 538n.

for alleviation and release. . . . And within the wide spectrum of emotions (replacing the simpler mask of ironic protestation) it is among those poems where a tone of patience and a growing chorale of self-assurance prevails, that we find the lyrics of challenge to all who would deny her a place in this cherished realm of art. . . . And surely related to this is the fact that earlier her lyrics of captivity, of the cage, give way to celebrations of release, release not to be found in Heaven merely, but in the realm of poesy. . . . I wish to emphasise that this shift is simultaneous with the experience of bereavement, the result of her rejection, and has nothing to do with those poems projecting her death, or rendering her existence as death in life. . . .

(RE: TECHNICAL ANALYSIS)

But the most interesting phenomenon is the alteration of the form of the poetry itself . . ; there is a new conjoining of thought and feeling. . . .

Emily Dickinson added to her organic conception of form a new mode, the disjunctive structure. This consists of two or more simultaneously expanding metaphors, creating a double or even a multiple movement that required a new kind of reading. . . . One responds to this . . . with a willingness to take a leap across concurrent terms of an analogy. The value of such poetry is not the quality in the rendering of an idea but the manifestation of a new source of poetic power—the vitality that is generated in the reader.

Then again:

(RE: THE POET'S FUNCTION GENERALLY)

[p. 234] [in all her "poet poems"] she declares that the details of the real world are useful only as they enable the poet to render, by implication, the less apparent details of the unseen world; she explains to whoever would listen that the poet is a bard who sings of the relationship between the seen and the unseen. . . .

[p. 246] Because we inhabit the finite world we may share only the attributes of temporary reality, we must content ourselves with signs of the infinite. It is the business of the poet to recognize these signs. It is the business of the poet to observe

> transient phenomena and explain thereby the fixed universe, to confront jeopardy and prophesize safety. Eventually we will experience the transition between mortal life and eternal life, we will . . . voyage out of the limited circuit into the limitless circumference, and that which appalls momently will save finally. . . .
>
> There is one expanding metaphor drawn from the circuit world; it is conjoined (actually or by implication) to an equivalent metaphor drawn from the circumference world, and both are held in tension, bound together by juxtaposition not logic, perceived as related by a leap of the imagination not by fact, by intuition not reason.
>
> This poetic manner vitalizes a phrase or a line as easily as it enlivens a fully developed poem. . . .
>
> [p. 249] She accumulates her discoveries into a long link-poem that ultimately celebrates as it proclaims the relationship between the mortal and the immortal, the transient and the immutable, the finite and the infinite. . . .

Certainly Ruth Miller is not among those scholars who, pardonably befuddled and exhausted by the tormented and tormenting history of the MS publication, take the life-meaning out of Dickinson's work, in the way described by M. H. Williams. David Porter, in his second book on Dickinson, *The Modern Idiom*,[32] however, sadly, is:

> [p. 221] How conscious or precise her discriminating powers were is conjectural, for the triteness in her work sits side by side with the cutting raw poetic power and stunning psychological insight. . . .
>
> [p. 226] Like Hardy, but apparently less knowingly, her poetry was revolutionary because it avoided the jeweled line. . . .
>
> [p. 226] [in context of listing technical innovations: vernacular inserted in formal language; Anglo-Saxon vs. Latinate words; lexical set alien to subject; elided syntax, omitted transitions, dropped structural and syntactical copulas . . . which Porter calls discontinuity of structure and story]: [these] contribute to the powerful effect that is indubitably of our time: the es-

[32] Cambridge, MA: Harvard University Press, 1981.

trangement from outer reality and the resistance of common words to definitive meaning. . . .

[p. 232] The poems produce . . . that most modern of all attitudes, the ironicalization of experience. . . .

[p. 233] The tonal undercutting, the evasion of stock sincerity, the protective irreverence and throwaway understatement, thus making the hymn form play a different tune: all these effects, even if there were behind them no perspective of mind much more fundamental, would withal make Dickinson a modern. Neither sophisticated nor sustained, hers was a poetic cunning working by stealth of language and subversion of form to create surprise by strangeness. Out of these strategies came a disordering of experience, a new confession of our precarious status. . . .

[p. 236] Dickinson's radical endomodernism is found in her stroboscopic idiom which, lacking a structure of foreknowledge, effectively negated any totality of intent. Thus are produced the special problematics of her work: the lost referents, the sporadic incoherence and indeterminate meaning, the lack of self definition, the lost viewpoint. . . . With these particular circumstances of linguistic derangement, we are inside the modern dilemma. . . .

[p. 238] If we seek a field theory that connects her existence and her art it is this: her artful selection along the plane of lexical choice and her lack of sustained structure on the plane of combination exactly reflect the phenomenon of intensity without a cause. It is vertical linguistic power without cumulative direction. . . .

[p. 239] the void between desire and its fulfilment can only be filled by the language for that desire. . . .

[p. 240] The more the world receded before her protective rush of words, the more words were needed to make their self-sufficient world. . . . Language with Dickinson begins to break off its old kinship with the complicated exterior world and enters into a lonely sovereignty, to use Michel Foucault's words in a new reference, from which it reappears in its separated state as one kind of modern literature. Reality becomes impervious and what is put in its place, in reclusion from the world . . . is the poetic construction that is nondiscourse. The

> world then is only a remoteness that haunts the house of art. . . .
>
> [p. 253] Her texts display . . . the great modern question of the relationship of language and artistic imagination to reality. . . .
>
> [p. 254] We thus can see that the fragmentation of the Dickinson poetic canon—the brevity, the scraps, the impacted language, the intensity without development, the failure of wholeness—is the visible wrestling of her imaginative power with the problem of art without belief, without grace, without assent. . . . So in Dickinson, as in much later poetry, there are no radical similitudes, no representation, no organization beneath the self-promoting language. The defective mirror displays the disconnected images of a defective reality. . . .
>
> [p. 255] The result was that her language released itself from the strict architecture of syntax, from the architecture of thought, and thus from the architecture of reality. [This constituted] . . . the opening of the breach between reality and imagination.

It is distressing to witness such implicit despair regarding Dickinson's work and the function of poetry in general—a despair that is, however, the rather inevitable fruit of a mistaken, rigidly over-schematic use of the study of linguistics starting around the 1960s. It is also concomitantly the result of a *conceptual* failure in succeeding generations as to how carry forward this inheritance authentically, a failure to "[*have* this] new experience". And it is all the more remarkable in that Porter is one of the few scholars who initially had understood the importance of working with the poems with an idea of chronological order rather than falling into the trap of a haphazard, fragmentary view of them all in a confused, disparate mass, since his early volume was, precisely, a study of *The Art of Emily Dickinson's Early Poetry*. He was one of the few critics who mentioned Miller's thorough work, and perhaps the only critic she speaks well of in her 1968 study. Needless to say, there is no acknowledgement, and indeed no trace, of Miller's work in this second book.

7. "I will not let thee go except I bless thee." The sense of chronological development in verbal form

But the point is that, while a correct sense of the dating of the poems may emerge intuitively from immersion in Dickinson's work and operate implicitly in a method of reading the groups of poems in terms of typological or thematic linking, such a method may be premature. For what cannot thus be shown and indeed remains pure fanciful conjecture—if not prejudice—scientifically speaking, is how these forms of language developed in the first place, and indeed whether the linking assumed is authentic.

Furthermore, Dickinson's (I, too, believe) experimental linking may be just a further stage of composition, a growing elucidation of further "relations within relations". It may be part of the chronological development of meaning, the Idea, itself; even perhaps the gradual development of some modern equivalent of the epic form, that "first flower . . . of a new symbolic mode", as Langer describes it,[33] "not merely a receptacle of old symbols, but . . . a new symbolic form, great with possibilities, ready to take meanings and express Ideas that have had no vehicle before"; that "hodge podge of literary creations, vaguely yet grandly spanned by a story—the all-inclusive story of the world".[34] The pattern of Dickinson's work

---

[33] Langer, *Feeling*, 202.

[34] Ibid. She continues (p. 305): "It was probably the discovery that different poetic practices had different effects, causing various moods and movements in successive parts of the epic, that gave rise to the special literary forms. Each separate means of poetic creation could be exploited and gave rise to a genre of smaller scope but more organized form." In this context of the question of the rejuvenation of language and form, see *Holmes*, p. 145: "his instinct that the modern Epic subject must now centre on 'the mind of man', through 'travels, voyages and histories', shows a shift of poetic focus characteristic of the new Romantic age. The Epic could no longer draw on classic or religious mythology for the framework of its action. It must become contemporary with the world of scientific, anthropological, and psychological exploration: it must centre in some way on the drama of self-knowledge, on the growth of consciousness and civilisation". See in this connection, for example, Dickinson's L 348: "We meet no Stranger but Ourself"; L354: "the mind is such a new place, last night feels obsolete"; L555: "we cannot believe for each other. I suppose there are depths in every Consciousness, from which we cannot rescueourselves—to which none

may not so much consist in the thematic one of finding peace and resolution to suffering as in the impetus to discover a principle of infinite departures, in experience as in the linguistic form that enables it.[35]

Using such a preconceived thematic-grouping method, we cannot reliably deduce how the Idea developed as the forms progressed, such that they attain that vitalizing quality of "seeming new every time you look at them, inexhaustible",[36] such that they offer us the possibility of a "change of mind". If we wish to freeze Emily Dickinson into a god, against all her better advice, let us be intimidated by her forgivable vindictiveness and bow to I. N. Kher's dictate that "the manuscripts are undated and should be allowed to remain so".[37] We do no service to Emily Dickinson, and I am more inclined to the style of Bowles' irritation when, during a visit to the Homestead, he reputedly shouted at her hiding up-

---

can go with us—which represent to us Mortally—the Adventure of Death—How unspeakably sweet and solemn—that whatever await us of Doom or Home, we are mentally permanent."; PF 21: " As there are Apartments in our own Minds that . . . we never enter without Apology—we should respect the seal of others".

[35] My own idea, for example, would be that the poems progressed through groups expressing development as follows:

1. Ingenuous joy—primary innocence;
2. Simple pain—observation of death, not suffered in person—identification with "she"/mother figure;
3. Love—having/losing it—"he" poems—ecstasy/pain—pleading little girl persona—anger with Christ/Master;
4. Crushing pain (on not possessing the object entirely)—experienced generally and in relation to "he"—destruction the principle of life—enraged searching for the principle of life—despair;
5. Bearing it—hitting back—sarcasm—the search for real courage;
6. Maturer love—broken objects coming into integral focus—development of Self—acknowledging of need—learning—relinquishment of dependence as "love"—desire to serve—capacity to wait;
7. Observation—maturer, less intrusive investigation—recuperation of wonder/complex pain—love of earth/knowledge of its immanent loss—remorse at death of "father" in growth of self, recognition of its inevitability—not destruction, progression.

But presently it remains only an idea, perhaps a preconception.

[36] Langer, *Philosophy*, 239.

[37] See *The Landscape of Absence*, New Haven, CT, 1974, 275, n. 13.

stairs: "'Emily, you damned rascal! No more of this nonsense! I've traveled all the way from Springfield to see you. Come down at once.'" Sewall continues: "Down she came, we are told, and was charming and sociable. (Clearly, she needed more Bowlses in her life.)"[38]

It is as well to state explicitly that I cannot agree with Vivian Pollak's view (*Dickinson: The Anxiety of Gender*, Ithaca, NY: Cornell University Press, 1984, 22), that: "[Dickinson's] art exhibits no clear-cut psychological development; she has no early, middle and late manner"; and that furthermore, the claim to congruence that Pollak intimates between this view, and Northrop Frye's, when Frye states that "[Dickinson] seems, after her early valentines, to have reached her mature style almost in a single bound" (in ed. Perry Miller et al., *Major Writers of America*, 2 vols., New York: Harcourt Brace and World, 1962) seems to me very forced. In this connection: Johnson, in his Introduction to *Emily Dickinson: The Complete Poems* (London: Faber and Faber, 1970) states that: "The increasing momentum [of Dickinson's creativity] after 1860 reached its peak in 1862 and sustained its full power for three more years"; whereas it would seem more correct to estimate her development from the *quality* of the linguistic form. Anyone who reads the letters cannot but be struck by the dramatic change in Dickinson's use of language with the years, and by the ever subtler, osmotic boundaries between their poetic prose and formal poems. In qualitative terms, they never look back (for example, L868 to Sue Dickinson on Gilbert's death in 1883, and only three years before her own, is forcefully poetic: so is L873, to name but two), undergoing a period of very terrible "jostling" (L901 & P1100), probably round about the period of the "Master" letters, which inevitably brings to mind her images of herself out on the sea without a keel, perhaps with a fin (though not always that), "guessing the waters" (L822), treading them to show a friend the way (L306), buffeting the Breeze and looking into the white-light-air, "conjecturing a form of space" (L790)—and with these, of course, the image of the "wrestler on the spar" (P201, L967), and the potential transforming despair (and ecstasy) in that.

---

[38] Sewall, *Life*, 510.

We are interested in Dickinson's "reasonableness and humanity". "The mind in creation", Shelley tells us,[39] "is as a fading coal, which some invisible influence, like an inconstant wind, awakens to transitory brightness. . . . It is as it were the interpenetration of a diviner nature through our own; but its footsteps are like those of a wind over the sea, which the coming calm erases, and whose traces remain only, as on the wrinkled sand which paves it".

Surely it is important to be able to follow the "traces" of the chronological development of her poetic language, allowing interpenetrating illumination between this and the facts of her life. And this not in order to crack open her private affairs (surely substantially no different from our own), a possibility that she probably rightly feared as potentially damaging to the generative impetus of her art. But in order to understand how on earth she, unlike even perhaps many of the most talented of us, developed her unusual "power to conceive invisible realities", which is the function of genius;[40] how she managed to come to use her experience to create these life-symbols, to re-vitalize language, through which we may be enabled to "formulate our conceptions of feeling and our conceptions of visual, factual, and audible reality together . . . to clarify and organize intuition itself."[41] For if Langer is right in her thesis, that: "it is a mistake to think genius is complete from the beginning. Talent is much more likely to be so, wherefore the infant prodigy is a well-known phenomenon. Genius, indeed, sometimes appears only with maturity, as in Van Gogh, whose early pictures are undistinguished, and grows and deepens from work to work . . . long after technical mastery has reached its height", it begs the question even more. We need to understand what development these forms conveyed in Dickinson's mentality, in her idea of human sentience. Only this will show the "meaningfulness of her poetic activity", enable us to attain what Coleridge termed the "*intellectual* comprehension" that will give it "perma-

---

[39] In *A Defence of Poetry*, in *Shelley's Prose*, ed. David Lee Clark, London: Fourth Estate, 1988, 275–298. There are many apparent echoes of this essay in Dickinson's work, though Shelley here is using Coleridge's vocabulary ("interpretation") built out of the German influence. For examples of Dickinson's own, analogous evocations of inspiration and its expression, see L190, L265, L271, L319, L405, L937.

[40] Langer, *Feeling*, 409.

[41] Ibid., 397.

nence". And this, in the last resort, once the symbol is duly imparted, is no longer exclusively the business of Emily Dickinson as a person, nor the exclusive business of the relatives, nor of the copyright holders nor of the acclaimed critics. It is the business of all persons who are genuinely *interested* in it.[42]

---

[42] Coleridge, *Notebooks*, III, 3910. In this context, it is difficult not to remember some of the concluding observations and their concomitant hypotheses elicited and launched to posterity so movingly by Wilkinson & Willoughby in what they indeed modestly call their "Introduction" to Schiller's *Aesthetic Education* (p. cxcvi, see note 14 above): that "some of the heart-burnings [Schiller] experienced about the inferiority of philosophical activity [during the period of collaboration with Goethe when he was engaged on writing the treatise, but also receiving instalments of *Wilhelm Meister* in creation] was due, not just to the fact that Goethe was being poetically productive while he himself was still struggling to complete the series of theoretical works provoked by his study of Kant, but *by the actual content* [my emphasis] of Goethe's novel . . . For here, in the expansiveness of the epic form, it was possible to present . . . , with all the concrete uniqueness of the individual case, a whole panorama of the relations between life and art, the aesthetic and the moral, between semblance, true, false and misplaced . . . . All this may sound as though we thought that the chief challenge of Schiller's treatise is to scholars of various kinds. This is, of course, not the case at all. Its challenge is to any person, parent, or pedagogue who can read its message aright. And there must be many who have read it aright and acted upon it. Acting upon it, moreover—whether successfully or unsuccessfully—is a very real factor in its right interpretation. For . . . though not arrived at by purely empirical means, his propositions are to be tested operationally . . . each new interpretation provokes a new kind of testing, and each kind of testing works back upon interpretation. Schiller more than once voiced the opinion that these *Letters* were the best thing he had ever done, or was capable of doing, and that they would constitute his claim to immortality." This insight, born of such articulate logical clarity, into the deeply disturbing and often unbearably painful, if exhilarating, quality of genuinely aesthetic work and the explosiveness of the impact of the subject with "beauty"—such that the recurrent escape into multifarious forms of less demanding, or even perverse, experience should not surprise—seems rare, and of great importance, to me. For it is certainly central to Dickinson's work, and to our studies of this, where the lack of such a "concept", if this is an adequate term for the illuminating constellation of particular points, seems often to have led to much of the misunderstanding regarding, for example, the nature of Dickinson's "renunciation", "isolation", "abnormality", and so on (parallel to the cynical judgement of Schiller's pain as symptomatic of gnawing envy of his friend, rather than the courageous opening to ravishment at the intricate and comprehensive beauty of such creation). What other excuse can one possibly adduce

Emily Dickinson hypersensitively thwarted our attempts to study the biography of the poems, but she left the door ajar with the dated letters, which over the years became so extraordinarily powerful linguistically, so pictorial of and integral to the process of her wrestling to compress language into significant metaphor, as sometimes to be more truly poetic than the verses themselves, which can sometimes seem banal out of a wider context. This present study is dedicated to trying to show that the attempt to scientifically map the development of the poetic language via the dated letters is a viable undertaking, and to show the seamless relationship this language has to the poems. Future work will be dedicated to attempting to apply these findings to the poems, in order to deduce their chronology internally.

---

for forms of argument such as that Dickinson was "imperfectly socialized, which explains why she was always in love" (Vivian R. Pollak, *Dickinson: The Anxiety of Gender*, Ithaca and London: Cornell University Press, 1984, 51)? Even were it true, and not just fiction in the premise leading to fiction in the deduction, one would be at a loss to see its use. We know that nearly all her copious correspondence with Otis Phillips Lord was destroyed after her death, and that the slivers that remain, beautiful and artistically mature as indeed they are, were brutally edited almost out of existence. Are we really going to continue for the next twenty years believing that Dickinson did not go to live with Lord because she had decided it was best to renounce the experience of intimate passionate relationship and the attempted expression of this, which is, indeed, a kind of "farewell" hope, gift, and tribute to those who come after? Also see note 67 below, and Appendix B.

II

The aesthetic: "Keeping believing nimble"

> On subjects of which we know nothing, or should I say *Beings*— . . . we both believe, and disbelieve a hundred times an Hour, which keeps Believing nimble.
>
> L750, to Otis Phillips Lord, 30 April 1882

> The numerals of Eden do not oppress the student long, for Eden ebbs away to diviner Edens
>
> L645, to Otis Phillips Lord,
> date unknown: officially conjectured about 1880

I shall now present a pilot version for a research into the development of thought and technique in Dickinson's poetic language. I have here worked centrally with the extant letters, using for the backbone of the study those that can be dated with certainty.

I give the full text of three letters and detailed comment on them (Sections 1, 2, 3), showing links between these and other material where relevant, as the shifts from one image to another, broadening her network of metaphor and selecting a language, and the changes in the structure of her syntax, show the development and becoming of her thought. I then follow this with a paradigm of my findings. It is my opinion that these findings are rich enough to encourage a full-scale research into the letters, through which to develop a periodic table for the evolution of her use of poetic diction. Upon this armature, it should be possible to arrange the poems sequentially and ultimately to make Dickinson's work available for aesthetic research—that is, for exploration into the genesis of an aesthetic object, as described above.

Originally I made a short-list of about 50 letters of certain dating, scattered over the arc of her life. From a continual re-reading of these, I eventually selected three, each some ten years from the earlier one, not—as far as possible—on the basis of preconception as to the kind of changes in the language I might seek confirmation of, but rather on the basis of an intuition of each one having a quality typical to a different phase in her writing. I then attempted a close reading of each of these, firstly to build an idea of the kind of work required of the recipient in relating to the communication, and secondly to open out a receiving net in which I might compare retrospectively the possible different uses of images, metaphors, syntactical structures, vocabulary, punctuation, rhythms, idioms, sources and modes in her language as she progressed.

1. Imitating form in the 1850s

> I have had some things from you, to which I perceived no meaning. They were either very vast, or they did'nt mean anything. I dont know certainly which.
>
> (L152, to Austin Dickinson, January 5 1854)

Letter 50, 19 August 1851, to Abiah Root

(I have numbered lines in all three letters, to facilitate reference to commentary)

"Yet a little while I am with you, and again a little while and I am not with you" because you go to your mother! Did she not tell me saying, "yet a little while ye shall see me and again a little while and ye shall not see me, and I would that where I am, there ye may be also"—but the virtue of the text consists in this my dear—that "if I go, I come again, and ye shall be friend where I am;" that is to say, that if you come in November you shall be mine, and I shall be thine, and so on "vice versa" until "ad infinitum" which isn't a great way off! While I think of it my dear friend, and we are upon these subjects, allow me to remark that you have the funniest manner of popping into town, and the most lamentable manner of popping out again of any one I know.

It becomes to me a matter of serious moment, this propensity of your's concerning your female friends—the "morning cloud and the early dew" are not more evanescent.

I think it was Tuesday evening that we were so amused by the oratorical feats of three or four young gentlemen—I remember I sat by you and took great satisfaction in such seat and society—I remember further our mutual Goodnights, our promises to meet again, to tell each other tales of our own heart and life, to seek and find each other after so long a time of distant separation—I can hardly realize Abiah that these are recollections, that our happy today joins the great band of yesterdays and marches on to the dead—too quickly *flown* my Bird, for me to satisfy me that you *did* sit and sing beneath my chamber window. I only went out once after the time I saw you—the morning of Mr Beecher, I looked for you in vain—I discovered your Palmer cousins, but if you indeed were *there* it must have been in a form to my gross sense impalpable. I was *disappointed* Abiah—I had been hoping much a little visit from you—when will the hour *be* that we shall sit together and talk of what we were, and what we *are* and may be—with the shutters *closed*, dear Abiah and the balmiest little breeze stealing in at the window? I *love* those little fancies, yet I would love them *more* were they not *quite so fanciful* as they have seemed to be—I have fancied so many times and so many times gone home to find it was *only* fancy that I am half afraid to *hope* for what I *long* for. It would seem my dear Abiah that out of all the moments crowding this little world a *few* might be vouchsafed to spend with those we love—a *separated* hour—an hour more pure and true than *ordinary* hours, when we could *pause* a moment before we journey on—we had a *pleasant* time talking the other morning—had I known it was *all my portion*, mayhap I'd *improved* it more—but it never'll come back again to try whether or no. Dont you think sometimes these brief imperfect meetings have a tale to tell—perhaps but for the sorrow which accompanies *them* we would not be reminded of brevity and change—and would build the dwelling *earthward* whose site is in the skies—perhaps the treasure *here* would be *too dear* a treasure—couldn't "the moth corrupt, and the thief break thro' and steal"—and this makes me think how I *found* a little moth in my stores the other day—a very *subtle* moth that had in ways and manners to me and mine unknown, contrived to hide itself in a favorite worsted basket—how long my little treasurehouse had furnished an arena for it's destroying labors it is not *mine* to tell—it had an errand there—I trust it *mine* to tell—I trust it fulfilled it's mission; it taught me dear Abiah to have no treasure *here* or rather it tried to tell me in it's little mothy way of another *enduring* treasure, the robber cannot steal which, nor time waste away. How many a lesson learned from lips of such tiny teachers—dont it make you think of the Bible—"not many mighty—not wise"?

You met our dear Sarah Tracy after I saw you here—her sweet face is the same as in those happy school days—and in vain I search for wrinkles brought on by many cares—we all love Sarah dearly, and shall try to do all in our power to make her visit happy. Is'nt it very remarkable that in so many years Sarah has changed so little—not that she has stood still—but has made such peaceful progress—her thot's tho' they are older have all the charm of youth—have not yet lost their freshness, their innocence and peace—she seems so pure in heart—so sunny and serene, like some sweet lark or Robin ever soaring and singing—I have not seen her much—I want to see her more—she speaks often of you, and with a warm affection—I hope no change or time shall blight these loves of ou [r]'s, I would bear them all in my arms to my home in the glorious heaven and say "here I am my Father, and those whom thou hast given me." If the life which is to come is better than dwelling here, and angels are there and our friends are glorified and are singing there and our friends are glorified and are singing there and praising there need we fear to go—when spirits beyond wait for us—I was meaning to see you more and talk about such things with you—I want to know your views and your eternal feelings—how things beyond are to you—Oh there is so much to speak of in meeting one you love, and it always seems to me that I might have spoken more, and I almost always think that what was found to say might have been left unspoken.

Shall it always be so Abiah—is there no longer day given for our communion with the spirits of our love?—writing is brief and fleeting—conversation will come again, yet if it will, it hastes and must be on it's way—earth is short Abiah, but Paradise is long there must be many moments in an eternal day—then sometime we shall tarry, while time and tide roll on, and till then Vale!

Your own dear
Emilie.

The letter opens with a long, exuberant play on a quotation from *John* (16:16), far more complicated and heavy with words than the essence of her meaning—if such an 'essence' exists. On the one hand she seems to be saying that she misses Abiah, but that parting should not mean parting forever; on the other hand she seems to be conveying a tangle of unconsidered feelings that collapse into bitterness and hurt, and attempting to avoid these. Whatever the genuine feeling is, it is quite drowned by the language. Rather she is obviously enjoying the riddling use of words and the apparent paradox created in the Biblical statement by the acrobatic use of so few verbs—go, come, be; and she is also tasting transgression—for example, her substitution of the Bible's "Father" with "mother". She then puts what are presumably common turns of speech, for their Latin-ness, on a par with Biblical quotations—"vice versa", "ad infinitum". The "infinitum" takes her to infinity, to eternity, to Immortality "which isn't a great way off", and again, when she draws the threads of this spinning paragraph together with a cosmetically rhetorical device that would pretend to be opening a new topic ("While I think of it . . .", l. 10), she takes the Bible's grand solemnity home and puts it in the drawing-room in "lamentable" (*John* 16:20). But all this is like dancing on top of meaning, not entering it.

In the second paragraph, the word games become less thick and fast, slipping ever closer to an expression of hurt and bitterness at Abiah's absence; and she gives one last display in the linking of an otherwise rather nebulous trio—morning cloud, early dew and her "female friend"—through the word "evanescent", a word that became heavy with meaning later.

With "I think it was Tuesday evening" (l. 19), the riddling falls away, and it is almost as if "up comes little memory and paints and paints" (L77) to use the metaphor she often does, in one form or another, in the context of realizing a separation from someone she is fond of, and that already seems to suggest the link between the departed beloved and the impulse to write that we will see become ever more urgent later. But here the painting doesn't last long or go very deep: it begins in a decorous, sentimentally Victorian style, with the girls sitting listening to the "oratorical feats of three or four young gentlemen" (l. 20). (There's perhaps a grain more truth in her confession to Sue (L85): "I do think it's wonderful that our hearts dont break every day when I think of all the whiskers, and all the gallant men but I guess I'm made with nothing but a hard heart of stone, for it dont break any".)

The nascent images soon wind up to a pitch of petulant languishing: "our mutual Goodnights, our promises to meet . . . to tell . . . to seek . . .", accompanied by an exaggerated sense of time and distance: "so long a time of distant separation" (l. 25). After which, she sinks into a complaint against these portraits and then abandons them, on the grounds that they are not the real thing, are of the closed past, are "recollections", "join the great band of yesterdays and march on to the dead" after the fashion of some militantly Puritanical household where they stay buried and silenced forever. The suggestion behind the ensuing image of the "Bird too quickly flown" (l. 28), as it appeared as a catch-phrase in many other letters of this earlier period,[43] is the nightingale and at least partly that of Keats.[44] This image, linked to (winged) angels, will reappear frequently in the context of the sudden disappearance of people dear to her,[45] and link to a network of metaphor that I discuss particularly in Section II.3. Here the phrase and subsequent detail of the bird that may, or may not, have sat within earshot are a memory of the *Ode to a Nightingale*. But while Keats' experience of the bird leaves him with a sense of separation, loss, and ongoing thought (which I mention because it becomes a theme for Dickinson), but not in revolt against the experience of her song, Dickinson's use of the situation (for it is not developed into working metaphor), full of reproach not enquiry, seems to suggest that, if the bird was a dream it was so in the fatuous sense of the word and not in the sense she uses it later (more as "fiction"),[46] and probably it was not even that—probably the bird really *did not* sit below her Julietlike chamber window at all. The interest lies in that Dickinson's use of her source here diminishes the original, whereas later her use of 'sources' did not. Here the symbol of the nightingale sits divested of its power to become, as it were, part of

---

[43] E.g. L39, L154, L173, L175.

[44] See Appendix A: Dickinson and Keats: some notes on influence and affinity.

[45] E.g. L39, L204, L671, L779.

[46] E.g. L330, L653.

that "cyclic poem written by Time upon the memories of men" (Shelley, *Defence of Poetry*). Dickinson continued to work with other writers' words and the "pauses" between them—though she was not a name-dropper, as Higginson found to his irritation—but this changed in her style, and she grew to wrestle with the whole portent of the writings that haunted her mind.

The reproachful narrative continues with her describing the sacrifices that define her own fidelity and distinguish it from her friend's neglect (*she* had only gone out *once* since they'd met); and the ironical naming of Abiah's "form to my gross sense impalpable" (ll. 33–34), Miltonic in syntax and vocabulary, is, once again, a tribute to her imitative powers but a mere game with words, more in the concealing nature of what Coleridge would have called an "abstraction",[47] at a further remove from, rather than an intensification of, actual meaning ('Abiah was not there'). This lapses back again into a rhapsodic nostalgia and slips, as it were unintentionally into what seems to me the first authentic image of the letter (ll. 35–36): "When will the hour be that we shall sit together and talk of what we were— . . . with the shutters closed, dear Abiah and the balmiest little breeze stealing in at the window". The atmosphere evoked is—here unintentionally—tomblike and stifling, rather like one aspect of her later, very complex, "Alabaster chambers" (P216). It seems to be picked up again later poetically, as nothing else in the letter is, in the "moth corrupting and the thief breaking through and stealing" (ll. 57–58): both by "steal", which becomes a pun ("stealing in"), and in the implication of a tightly-sealed secret place where some enviable treasure is hidden (their friendship), which, as it were in line with its magnetic flaunting of intent to remain inviolable, becomes prey to envious thieves. Again, these suggestions of secrecy and "clandestineness",[48] as signs of life's mystery and essential beauty, became ideas that never left her, but they changed their quality and context later. That is, from involving a sort of stolen idealized perfection that shut life out (which meant all but the hapless elect, who got

[47] *The Statesman's Manual*, 1816, *Lay Sermons*, ed. R. J. White, London: Routledge & Kegan Paul, 1960, 30–31.

[48] L354: "Life is the finest secret. So long as that remains, we must all whisper. With that sublime exception I had no clandestineness."

ceremoniously laid one by one in her "box of Phantoms" anyway), the idea shifted to a kind of battle with herself (the "skirmish in my mind", L743). The "infinite beauty" (that she felt she had to flee from later, L319) had to be "waited for", as the lady asks to "wait for" the "Master" in L233. Life had to be allowed to happen without "meddling" (L893) with it through "ravenousness", "clamour for its loveliness", (L643, L824) or anything else, except in metaphor, which—though she forever felt a certain ambivalence towards it—she came to value as a possible form of holding power that *may*, appropriately used, encourage and enable the furthering of understanding and progression of truthful living meaning and form.

"I love those little fancies" (l. 39) withdraws from the picture-painting again and for a moment exposes the contradictoriness of her own problem: she is always disappointed by the disparity between what she hopes for and reality, and yet she persists with the same unaltered hopes and fancies. "I am half afraid to hope for what I long for" (l. 43)—is it possible to "long" without "hoping"? The meanings of the words have some essential area of overlap, and yet she would make them distinct. Moving into a comfortably grandmotherly tone ("It would seem my dear Abiah"), she speculates on a better system for external reality than the existing one (the "separated . . . more pure and true" hour where we could "pause"), which she then contrasts specifically and rather touchingly to the transience of her meeting with Abiah: "Had I known it was all my portion, mayhap I'd improved it more" (l. 50). This last phrase has the same quality of breaking its logical possibilities as the "longing" that isn't "hoping" before had. And although these are in a very straightforward context here—she tries to make her language express propositional thought—it seems the beginnings of the search for "Circumference", the house of "possibility",[49] the

[49] See, for example, L268 to Higginson: "My Business is Circumference". Paul Ferlazzo (*Emily Dickinson*, Boston, Twayne, 1976) suggests she got the term from Emerson's essay "Circles". In fact Shelley (*Defence of Poetry*) uses the terms "centre" and "circumference", which she, like so many others and not only in the English literature, often counterposed: "Poetry is indeed something divine. It is at once the centre and circumference of knowledge." The idea of these is dynamic in many, many other images of Dickinson's, for example: "An enlarged ability for missing is perhaps a part of our better growth, as the

superficial contradictions contained in ambiguous forms of words such as: "I explore but little since my mute Confederate"; "this plank of Balm"; "We thank thee Oh Father for these strange Minds, that enamor us against thee"; "the treason of Progress, that dissolves as it goes" (L319, L390, L472, L280).

She shuts the lid on this phantom ("but it never'll come back again to try whether or no", l. 51) and, taking a step back from her personal pain, moves into what seems to me the core of the letter: "Dont you think sometimes these brief imperfect meetings have a tale to tell—perhaps but for the sorrow which accompanies them we would not be reminded of brevity and change". But after a dash—more expressive of uncertainty as to where to go than creative of that ambiguity or force of meaning that becomes so significant in her technique later—this backfires into an orthodox piece of moralizing ("and we would build . . .") of the sort she was to challenge as long as she lived.[50] Her considerations on the moral,

---

strange Membranes of the Tree broaden out of sight" (L951), and Shelley uses this image in the same passage as well. For "possibility" see, e.g., P657. Like the "circumference", it links ideally to many other metaphors, such as "boundlessness" (L381).

[50] Cf., for example, Dickinson's L271 to Higginson, enclosing, with irony to the point of cruelty, the poems "Before I got my Eye put out" and "I cannot dance upon my Toes", August 1862: "Are these more orderly? I thank you for the Truth—I had no Monarch in my life, and cannot rule myself . . . I suppose the pride that stops the Breath, in the Core of Woods, is not of Ourself—You say I confess the little mistake, and omit the large—Because I can see Orthography—but the Ignorance out of sight—is my Preceptor's charge—. . . When much in the Woods as a little Girl, I was told that the Snake would bite me, that I might pick a poisonous flower, or Goblins kidnap me, but I went along and met no one but Angels, who were far shyer of me, than I could be of them, so I hav'nt that confidence in fraud which many exercise". It is interesting to compare this to Wilfred Bion's observation: "I am myself struck by the toughness of what we call 'conscience'. It has been remarked, conscience makes cowards of us all. So it does. It is one of the really vital bullies which is difficult to bring under any control. For one thing, it is so moral. Anybody who poses the free play of morality is by that very fact sinning. In certain religions people talk about 'original sin'. Freud talks about 'free-floating guilt'. It has a long history—long before anybody managed to attach an articulate label to it. . . . It is a great sin for somebody to enjoy themselves. If he had a few months of happiness . . . somebody would be sure to suffer . . . " (*Bion in New York and São Paolo*, Perthshire, Scotland: Clunie Press, 1980, 71).

however, do not sit so prettily: she puns on the word "dear", suggesting we might grow happily fond of an earth-built treasure (incurring God's jealousy, much exalted in the Old Testament but increasingly less so by her); and that it might cost too much (this linked to its other "dear"-ness), both of which hinge on the possibility of destruction in the moth/thief breaking through and corrupting/stealing image. And as I said before, this image seems to throw back on the earlier closed-shuttered, perfect room (the treasurehouse) as the inevitable reason why that degree or quality of closeness is not externally either possible, nor perhaps even desirable. It invites its own destruction.

At this point the tone of the letter goes crazy: the symbolic moth suddenly becomes a real insignificant little moth and the treasurehouse a worsted basket, and the metaphor becomes literal, making it very funny (often what happens to metaphors if they are distorted back into that dimension). Partly this is her humorousness here, a deflating of the pomposity of her moralizing and insincere over-seriousness carried within a powerful technique of transformation of conventional images or statements, that we will meet again later in a much more committed form.[51] But it is partly an accidental lightness that simply relieves her from the difficulty of solving the problem of the "brief imperfect meeting"—a gift of a phrase for which she had some lovely variants later—and it soon gets clapped back into the simplistic, moralizing channel of less resistance: ("it taught me dear Abiah to have no treasure here", ll. 65–66)—something nobody ever managed to teach her actually), that of the automatically obedient Puritan schoolgirl—this time,

---

[51] See, for example, her humorous "Unless we become as Rogues, we cannot enter the Kingdom of Heaven" [L715], the "rogue" giving new life to the turgidness of the Biblical saying where, through endless moralistic repetition, the "children" hardly seem like children any more. Or the "Hock at my Lip" (PF66) that adds a sensuous enjoyment to its source in Psalm 23. Or the image of the "angel, with its needle, toiling beneath the snow" (L435) that links a whole network of images she works with (the needle of darning domestic hands that keep the shattered soul together, or perhaps the sailor's needle that "knows the North", the snow of mortified states, the ground where the anguished gardener tills in search of lost friends) and gives a highly original aspect to the "angel"—all part of what she called "Uncle Emily's ardor for the lie" (L315).

however, with a rather uncomfortable inversion of the Biblical reference, as if, like the obedience, it were squashed in at the last minute, when the syntax was already flowing in another direction: "it tried to tell me . . . of another enduring treasure, the robber cannot steal which, nor time waste away."

This moralizing does not take her very far, and she switches to muse enquiringly on the idealized portrait of the girl who has "made such peaceful progress" (ll. 77–78), as Sewall suggests,[52] probably wondering how such a thing as peaceful progress might be possible. In fact, the syntax of the sentence suggests ambivalence to the picture: "Sarah has changed so little", adding concessively and betraying the doubt: "—not that she has stood still". The "sweet Lark or Robin ever soaring and singing" image, like the earlier "morning cloud and early dew" or the oratorical gentlemen, is rather slippery and romanticizing (not the case with her bird and flower images in later contexts);[53] one cannot help feeling it has to do with the fact that she "hasn't seen her much". It is immediately followed, like the worsted basket by the moth, by the fear that "[some] change or time will blight these loves" and by the reiterated expression of what she longs for but dare not realize as hope, in the quotation from *John*: "here am I my Father". This is both affectionate and yet it is also an attempt, like the romanticizing imagery, to dispel the conflict she has come up against in her hurt over Abiah's unpermitted absence and her doubt as to whether peaceful Sarah Tracy was really progressing or rotting away statuesquely.

But it is not more than an attempt, for her doubts are ever lurking ("I would bear . . ." [l. 66]—the conditional implies impossibility) and resurge ("If the life which is to come . . ."): why, if as the rules of religion, patriotism, and good behaviour tell her, heaven is a better place and we all go there if we do the right thing and our friends are there in an idealized state ("glorified")—that is, they will have time for us—why should we be unwilling to die? But we are. This, it emerges, is what she needed time to discuss with Abiah—hardly a topic for pure, sunny, serene conversation in

---

[52] Sewall, *Life*, 372.

[53] See L 778, November 1882, just after her mother's death, for an extreme case: "a Bird herself, she requires no Symbol".

a peaceful hour with the shutters closed and a balmy breeze stealing in at the window, after all. Then another core of genuine expression breaks through: "Oh there is so much to speak of in meeting one you love, and it always seems to me that I might have spoken more, and I almost always think that what was found to say might have been left unspoken". I take this as a critique of her own letter, of her impulse and capacity for expression at this stage, and it is worth considering in the light of her search for the "chiefest words" (L873).

She was to re-cast the same feeling towards the end of her life: "Perhaps Affection has always one question more which it forgot to ask"; "Had we less to say to those we love, perhaps we should say it oftener, but the attempt comes, then the inundation, then it is all over, as is said of the dead" (L773, L962). And she uses the same image as this last to describe the flooding of affection (perhaps related to the "little force exploding", L271) many times, but in particular round about the same period (1882–85): "The Spirit never twice alike, but every time another—that other more divine. Oh had I found it sooner! But Tenderness has not a Date—it comes—and overwhelms" (L750). Earlier she plays with the term "enough": "Many write that they do not write because they have too much to say—I, that I have enough"; "Enough is so vast a sweetness I suppose it never occurs. . . . Even the Possible has it's insoluble particle" (L293, L352). Seen together, these seem to suggest something about her experiment with her art. It is Affection that generates the will to communicate; but the problem is not generation of quantity as such (there is too much and too little at the same time) but of solving that "enough" that is 'perfection'. The problem, like the problem of the "chiefest" words, is of quality, of finding the form that is adequate to its object.

To Emily Dickinson, the gesture of communication, the desire to communicate through language, was an act of love, an act of fundamental searching appreciation of the other being, and as such it had to be truth-ful, to reach constantly for that "more" or "enough" that was trying to get nearer to the truth. Because of these conditions and the limits (what Coleridge called "defects") of language,[54] what the words capture in their form is never that

---

[54] *Notebooks*, III, 3312.

thing that the speaker was striving to express: not enough and too much. And perhaps the increasingly poetic quality of the prose of her letters is directly linked to this necessity of finding the "chiefest" words, a shape of words capable of truth-fulness, as she obviously felt this letter was not. Perhaps a poetic shape of words can catch in the different spaces made by the particular relationship of one "chief" word to another, that "more" that prose, with its usually linear, consecutively rational and so partial properties can not, and in this sense enable that "communion with the spirits of our love" for which she so yearned.

One wonders whether she ever changed her mind about her final (in this letter) weighing up of two major modes of communication: "writing is brief and fleeting—conversation will come again, yet if it <u>will</u>, it hastes and must be on its way—". They seem antithetical—or if congruent only in their unsatisfactory "fleetingness"—and yet why should writing not come again more than conversation? Early on in her career she seems to have complained of the meaninglessness of the distance her pen set between her and her addressee: she called written words mere "symbols traced on paper", saying that she "disdained this pen and waited for a <u>warmer</u> language" (L15 & L96). Later she was more compelled by their power and enigmaticness: "we bruise each other less in talking than in writing, for then a quiet accent helps words themselves too hard"; "I almost inferred from your accent you might come. . . . I would like to make no mistake in a presumption so precious—but a Pen has so any inflections and a Voice but one" (L332 & L470). In any case, for her at this point writing is obviously not enough; perhaps for her as a human being, not as poet, it never was, and words always remained in a certain sense "wiles" (L555) and the "thing" itself silent like the inaudible thanks and companionable Dog–god (L417 & L261). But then again one thinks of the great significance the "fiction" came to have for her, which I discuss in Sections II.3 and II.4, and it may be that just as the human being and the poet interact and change each other, and the word and the object (if we are experiencing and expressing our experience), she may have oscillated in her feelings about which was the real thing. After all, Cordelia didn't just "love, and be silent", she said it as well.

She finally contrasts earth and Paradise in terms of time—metaphors she uses in at least two of her poems and a transposition she often plays with (P301 & P1067, this last also included in L316) and goes on to end the letter in a slightly nonsensical jingling manner.

So, generally, the first letter is bubblingly long-winded and devoid of any coherence of metaphor carrying concepts and developing thought or emotional power, though it is full of 'items': quotations, foreign turns of speech, Biblical stories, Puritan–Victorian settings, imitative literary structures. Contradictions in the relationship between words seem caused more by confusion than by complexity of meaning. It is gramatically correct, I would now say, in the sense of the correct "surface grammar" described by Meltzer as: "contain [ing] all those modifications of vocalization which the communication of information about the external world requires in order to minimize the many possible forms of ambiguity—and therefore confusion", but "notoriously poor for the communication of states of mind".[55] The letter is not poetically held together, it has no formal power; the essence of its communication is not in the words—which tend to be cumbersome—but seems to consist mainly in a complaint that breaks through sincerely now and then. The writer tries to solve the problems she raises in the complaint by falling back on a rather stereotyped moralizing and recourse to doctrine and is finally quite unsatisfied by the results. The letter does not end: it breaks down, it exhausts itself, and this is symptomatic of its lack of authentic poetic form. The kind of work required by the recipient is to chase along the words longitudinally, for they do not present any "self-regulating",[56] holding parameters of wider significance.

---

[55] See: "The Interaction of Visual & Verbal Language in Dreams", in *Language & Cognition: Essays in Honor of A. J. Bronstein*, New York: Raphael, 1983.

[56] For this term and its ramifications, see R. H. Stephenson, *Goethe's Conception of Science and Knowledge*, Edinburgh: Edinburgh University Press, 1995, pp. 14–15 and *passim* (henceforth *Goethe's Conception*) I am indebted to this rich, concise, fine, and forceful book for help in organizing and putting into focus some cardinal points concerning the "method of acquiring meaningful knowledge", as the author calls it in the Preface (with reference to Goethe). The Dickinson family library had two copies of Goethe's *Faust* (1859 and 1860 editions), and Schiller's *Works* (1853 edition). Given her intense interest in George Eliot and her admiration of her (then) courageous choice of life-style,

2. Revolutionizing form in the 1860s

Count not that far that can be had,
Though sunset lie between—
Nor that adjacent, that beside,
Is further than the sun.

L318, May 1866, to Mrs Holland

The second letter seems, in contrast, to have fragmented her language disturbingly. Full of tenses slightly out of true, structures that cram the separate words with ambiguities, a narrative line of apparently disjointed imagery and metaphor, dislocation of common idiom and a particularized punctuation, it had withal great force and seemed to imply a rather enigmatic internal organization of thought and feeling, in the sense of reference to a greater network of concepts and images between the lines. And in fact on close reading one can see the burgeoning of a particular language in the network of metaphors carrying a freight of particular meaning and enquiry, as one can see her relationship to literary or

---

and in people's lives and living forms generally, and given the way she read anything and as much as she could lay her hands on, Dickinson may well have read G. H. Lewes' 1856 biography of Goethe. See Sewall (*Life*, 570) for how quickly she got hold of Cross's life of Eliot on publication. And she was certainly acquainted at least with Margaret Fuller's translation of Bettina Brentano's published correspondence with Karoline von Günderode (see Rebecca Patterson, "Emily Dickinson's Debt to Günderode" in *The Midwest Quarterly*, VIII, 1967, 331–354). It also seems possible to me—from the new perspective that Richard Holmes' biography (*Early Visions*) has given on Coleridge's life and work, with a new sensitivity to what was authentically significant and positive in Coleridge's relationship to and transmission of German culture, far beyond the curiosity about his plagiarizing—that the more or less direct influence of these writers on Dickinson may have been significant. Coleridge's work was published and well known in America during Dickinson's lifetime. See also note 14 above. Some attention has been paid to the influence of Kant on Dickinson: see, for example, Frederick L. Morey ("Dickinson–Kant: The First Critique", in *Dickinson Studies*, Washington DC, 1986, 60, 1–70; "Dickinson–Kant, II (Covering the Second Critique, That of Practical Reason)", in *ibid.*, Washington DC, 1987, 64, 3–30; and "Dickinson–Kant, III: The Beautiful and the Sublime", in *ibid.*, 1988, 67, 3–60; "Dickinson–Kant, IV", in *ibid.*, 1990, 74, 1–61); by Linda Munk ("'Like Something Spiritual': A Brief Remark on Dickinson and Kant", in *ibid.*, 1992, 80, 27–28).

religious sources, to common speech, and indeed to common and occasional external events becoming increasingly complex as she absorbed and reacted to these and re-worked them in her new context.

Letter 235, Autumn 1861, to Mary Bowles

Mary.

I do not know of you, a long while—I remember you—several times—I wish I knew if you kept me? The Dust like the Mosquito, buzzes round my faith.

We are all human—Mary—until we are divine—and to some of us—that is far off, and to some [of] us—near as the lady, ringing at the door—perhaps that's what alarms—I say I will go myself—I cross the river—and climb the fence—now I am at the gate—Mary—now I am in the hall—now I am looking your heart in the Eye!

Did it wait for me—Did it go with the Company? Cruel Company—who have the stocks—and farms—and creeds—and it has just it's heart! I hope you are glad—Mary—no pebble in the Brook—today—no film on noon—

I can think how you look—You cant think how I look—I've got more freckles, since you saw me—playing with the schoolboys—then I pare the "Juneating" to make the pie—and get my fingers "tanned".

Summer went very fast—she got as far as the woman from the Hill—who brings the Blueberry—and that is a long way—I shall have no winter this year—on account of the soldiers—Since I cannot weave Blankets, or Boots—I thought it best to omit the season—Shall present a "Memorial" to God—when the Maples turn—

Can I rely on your "name"?

How is your garden—Mary? Are the Pinks true—and the Sweet Williams faithful? I've got a Geranium like a Sultana—and when the Humming birds come down—Geranium and I shut our eyes—and go far away—

Ask "Meme"—if I shall catch her a Butterfly with a vest like a Turk? I will—if she will build him a House in her "Morning—Glory". Vinnie would send her love, but she put on a white frock, and went to meet tomorrow—a few minutes ago. Mother would send her love—but she is in the "Eave spout", sweeping up a leaf, that blew in, last November. Austin would send his—but he dont live here—now—He married—and went East.

I brought my own—myself, to you and Mr. Bowles. Please remember me, because I remember you—Always.

My River runs to thee—
Blue Sea! Wilt welcome me?
My River waits reply—
Oh Sea—look graciously—
I'll fetch thee Brooks
From spotted nooks—
Say—Sea—
Take Me!

[Johnson's note: "Mary Bowles, now seven years old, was called 'Mamie' by her family, but Dickinson's spelling (l. 31) is clearly 'Meme'".]

The first thing it does is to dissuade the reader from trying to make sense of it by the logic of ordinary connections in grammar and imagery, by given, fixed connections between word and object. It portrays the difficulty in finding real meaning and, in its effort to do so, tries to establish a principle by which meaning may be sought. I hope what I mean by 'real' meaning and its distinction from 'fixed' meaning (which for Dickinson becomes equated with falsity or meaninglessness) will become clear in the course of the discussion, since this is an essential distinction in her work.

The straight vocative/imperative of the opening ("Mary")—something this letter has in common with the "Master" letters and a few others—immediately creates a sense of urgency and directness, as if sender and recipient were seeing "face to face".[57] Then we are plunged into tenses that do not fit the conventional phrases they seem they would form if they had not become "something

[57] I *Corinthians* 13:12: "For now we see through a glass darkly; but then face to face: now I know in part, but then shall I know even as also I am known". See also L15, L95, and particularly L93: "we have often touched upon [the subject], and as quickly fled away, as children shut their eyes when the sun is too bright for them", with reference to "noon" later in this L235.

else".[58] Various possible combinations of meaning pile up within the forms of the small groups of sentences, though they tend not to contain such intensely paradoxical contradictions and ambiguity as the later work that we shall see in the third letter. Unlike the first letter, where the best way to work was by describing it in different terms from without itself, the only option here is to work out from within the words.

"I do not know of you" initially seems to stand on its own, almost as if it were "I do not know you", giving the tone a hallowed, Biblically solemn feel. This is a register that continues throughout the letter on one level, as in the later "Can I rely on your 'name'?", emerging between the more 'familiar' images. Counterposed to "a long while" around the comma, it seems to conjure what would conventionally be a present perfect or simple past tense and the sense "hear about, from": "I haven't heard/ didn't hear from you for a long time". Then "I remember you"

---

[58] See L233: (second "Master" letter) for her use of this term, so particular and so general, as Coleridge said of "thing": " . . . I got tired holding him. I heard of a thing called 'Redemption'—which rested men and women. You remember I asked you for it—you gave me something else. I forgot the Redemption . . . ". It is interesting to compare it to a similar use in Donne: for example, in "The Relique": "Thou shalt be a Mary Magdalen, and I / A something else thereby"; or in *Aire and Angells*: "Still when, to where thou wert, I came, / Some lovely glorious nothing I did see", or in "The Legacie": "Yet I found something like a heart, / But colours it, and corners had", or the fourth stanza of the *Nocturnall upon S. Lucies Day*. The "disgrace" of the so-called 'Metaphysicals' in established literary circles in America in her day, as in ours until T. S. Eliot's rehabilitation of them, is—characteristically—unlikely to have cut much ice with Dickinson, who preferred to know things by "trying" them herself. Ruth Miller (*Miller*) gives some space to the issue; see also R. A. Thota and S. Singh, *Emily Dickinson: The Metaphysical Tradition*, Atlantic Highlands, NJ: Humanities, 1982. Some attention has been paid to her use of scientific metaphor, though this certainly also came in the wake of the European Romantic movement and links to her deep concern with methods of epistemological investigation: for example, by Daniel J. Orsini ("Emily Dickinson and the Romantic Use of Science" in *Massachussetts Studies in English*, Amherst MA, 1981, 7–8:4–1, 57–69); R. B. Sewall ("Science and the Poet: Emily Dickinson's Herbarium and 'The Clue Divine'", in the *Harvard Library Bulletin*, Cambridge, MA, Spring 1992, 3:1, 11–26); Fred D. White ("'Sweet Skepticism of the Heart': Science in the Poetry of Emily Dickinson", in *College Literature*, West Chester, PA, February 1992, 19:1, 121–128).

recalls the sense of "I don't know you" before, becoming a sort of antithesis on the one hand: "I do not know you: I remember you" (the hallowed register, face-to-face communication, the "cup where ecstasy is drunk", "infinite beauty comes too near to seek", L891, L319). On the other hand, around the dashes that here lend multiplicity of reference, it refers back to "a long while" and forward to "several times", and picks up its fixed, conventional tense and sense: "I've thought of you several times in this long while, I've been thinking about you for a long time". Then the dislocation of the tenses adjusts itself in the more self-contained "I wish I knew if you kept me", though this too could recollect "several times" at least. The choice of verb makes "me" sound like a photograph or token ("kept"—possessed) and in this context suggests "keeping in mind", recalling the earlier "I remember you" and its antithesis to "knowing you": all we "know" of another person is what we "remember", their face through our mind's eye, their photograph in the drawer of our mind ("Are not all Facts Dreams as soon as we put them behind us?, PF22). "Keep" also seems to evoke a sense of "keep faith", "observe", after the slightly ritualistic and sacred quality of the relationship that is building up: "I've lit a candle for you, Mary—have you for me?" And the tentative enquiringness explodes into a sure and sudden image: "The Dust like the Mosquito, buzzes round my faith". In what does its suddenness consist? Partly it is in the "Dust" coming out of nothing, followed hard upon by a simile that only makes the image less rather than more obvious (a simile usually just presents an image that displays the mechanism of something that is already essentially clear—for example, the classical Homeric one of men's lives being like the leaves on the trees, *Iliad*, vi.146). Why "Dust", then how is it "like the Mosquito"? Well, it "buzzes round my faith"—and the link is sealed. Somehow we must see it.

There remains an image of particles of dust, motes in the atmosphere, moving round a central object ("my faith"—perhaps a candle or sunbeam, suggesting an act of remembrance, the creation of the "Alive"). This draws in the mosquito then, and *vice versa*. My faith is like a bright attractive light that shows up the dust particles in the air until they seem to be circling round wilfully like mosquitoes. So perhaps faith (connected to "remembering") attracts dust—that is, forgetfulness (like the forgotten portrait gathering dust in the drawer) and so lack of faith, doubt, and this disturbs me, worries me, like a "buzzing" noise. Potentially there is doubt's death, as potentially there is the mosquito's inherent in its own attraction. But the "buzzing" signals the mosquito's life and endows the dust–doubt with a particularly aggressive quality, as if it could atttack mortally (not just irritate or alarm), rather like the "hand lightly created" that sends the letter-gun that "joggles the mind" as our reassuring "myths" (my "faith" in another aspect?) are put to the test.[59] "Dust" must also be connected, more traditionally, to mortals and mortality. In this connection, an image of "Motes" she uses later,[60] and which I discuss (see II.3), suggesting the living soul of the loved and sought "departed", might combine with the former to suggest both the dust–mote–immortal person (like the poet–letter writer) that upsets my "faith" (complacency) and might kill me if it does not "expand" me;[61] and yet it also suggests the fact of death that distracts me from my true faith, just as the buzzing fly of P465, which interposes instead of the King at the last telling moment, undermines such faith.

---

[59] See note 67 below regarding the "letter–gun". One aspect of her concept of "myth", a word that she uses in conjunction with "mote" in L937, P1062 (see text following, and note 60), seems similar to that expressed by the Nurse in Euripides' *Hippolytus*, l.198: "trusting to fables [Gk. "muthos"] we drift at random". The issue of the influence of the Classics on Dickinson has, in my view mistakenly, been little investigated. Ruth Miller (*Miller*, Appendix III, 390–392) has observed how, swayed by the prejudice that these could not have been important to her, Whicher and Johnson rejected three of the Dickinson family books on Classical literature presented to the Houghton Library by Gilbert H. Montague. A few later studies, however, include those by Persephone Tselentis-Apostolidis ("And I Will Be Socrates: Greek Elements in the Poetry of Dickinson", in *Dickinson Studies*, Washington DC, second half 1984, 52, 3–21); Diane Wakoski ("Emily Dickinson and Robert Creeley: Maverick Writers of the Latin Lyric", in the *New Orleans Review*, New Orleans LA, Spring 1992, 19:1, 14–26); Dennis L. Czerny ("'My Classics Vail Their Faces': Uncovering the Latin and Greek Elements in Emily Dickinson's Poetry", in *Dissertation Abstracts International*, Ann Arbor MI, December 1993, 54:6).

[60] Source in Milton, "Il Penseroso", l. 8, "gay motes that people the Sun Beams".

[61] See PF49 and my later discussion of this (Section II.3).

It is worth looking at P465 briefly, since it bears on the development of the images later in this letter as well.

I heard a Fly buzz—when I died—
The Stillness in the Room
Was like the Stillness in the Air—
Between the Heaves of Storm—

The Eyes around—had wrung them dry—
And Breaths were gathering firm
For that last Onset—when the King
Be witnessed—in the Room—

I willed my keepsakes—Signed away
What portion of me be
Assignable—and then it was
There interposed a Fly—

With Blue—uncertain stumbling Buzz—
Between the light—and me—
And then the Windows failed—and then
I could not see to see—

There seem two opposing tensions in it. One could read it as saying: "Instead of God the Father appearing as I left this life, there was the banality of a fly buzzing—though 'bluely' as if recalling the divine King's royalty?—and then: nothing. There is no God, no reason for faith." And this would be the aspect that concerns us here predominantly, I suspect. But one could also read it in the light of her remark (L294): "Death [is] as harmless as a Bee, except to those who run." That is: "Instead of that terrifying God Death coming along and frightening us out of our wits, there was a harmless little fly—uncertain, stumbling like an old man, but buzzing 'bluely'—and then it was like sleep". This possibility of the image of the fly–bee is interesting because it comes again—also latently—in the letter ("humming bird/Geranium and I shutting our eyes and going far away"), transformed into something congruent to this second aspect, if indeed this aspect is not already present in the Dust–mote–light–star possibility. Similarly, the "blue-buzz"—not in the letter as such but evidently in its shadow—is worth keeping in mind since it too seems to come up later in the "Blueberry" and "Blue sea", in connection with the discovery of the Beautiful/Royal/Eternal and the relation this seems to have to being "true" as the letter unfolds. Blue, of course, is traditionally the colour of faith/truth ("trawthe"), as in the pledge in Criseyde's "blewe ryng".[62]

"My faith", then, seems to refer to faith-in-the-afterlife and God-the-redeemer in the orthodox sense as in the poem, and as many of the terms in the letter do, and possibly to contain the criticism of the fixed, orthodox meaning as well (the suggestion of 'complacency', for example). More specifically, it refers to her doubt as to whether Mary "remembered" her, "kept" her in mind. It may also refer to her own forgetting and doubting, or forgetting-to-doubt (as when we become complacent: "Faith is Doubt" she was later to say, L912, 1884)—as it were "my faith to you": after the style of Herbert's allegorical dramatizations, her coat becomes covered wtih "dust and sin" as time passes, and dust gathers, obscuring the "kept" image.[63] And this may reflect on the slightly ambiguous quality of the first lines and to the sensation they give of her (infrequent) "remembering" of Mary, while always—inevitably—being marginally incongruent to "knowing" her, being totally so now.

The opening of the second paragraph ("We are all human") seems to gather together this sense of reciprocal doubt, as if to say initially 'nobody's perfect' or 'this is the state of being human—not knowing, forgetting . . .'. But then with the next clause—to which it is again ambiguously joined-yet-separated by the dashes—it seems to turn back on itself like the fly buzzing round our certainty: "—until we are divine" sounds almost a nonsense or platitude on one level, like saying 'we are all alive until we are dead' or 'a door is not a door when it is ajar'. And on one level it bears this nonsense or commonsense interpretation: 'We are all human (alive, unsafe and imperfect) until we are divine (dead,

[62] See "trawthe", for example, in *Sir Gawain and the Green Knight*, meaning "fidelity" (l. 626), "truth" (l.1050); but "plighted word" (ll. 1545, 1638, 1673) and "compact" (l. 2348), too. And Chaucer's *Troilus & Criseyde*, III, 885.

[63] "Love" (III), in *The Church*.

safe, and perfect in God).' But another sense in it seems to be 'we are all human except in those moments when we are divine'. And it is this that the letter continues to work on.

It is as if the time clause ("until we are divine") elicited the question "and when is that?"; "and to some of us", comes the answer, thereafter changing the "when" into "where", time into space (a transformation she often plays with, for she considered them both fictions). So to "some of us", being divine is "near" (could be any minute, is something that happens often), to some "far off" (will take long to acomplish, hardly ever happens). And what does she mean by "divine"? Again, the deeper, experimental aspect of the statement seems to pick up and sustain the deeper level of the letter: 'I do not know you—I remember you—do you remember me? I fear you don't, I fear I may have forgotten you; to fear and to be faithless is human'. To be "divine" must in some way be the opposite of these, perhaps close to "knowing" and coming "face to face"? Perhaps the strange series of images we're taken into at this point opens the issue out further.

Being divine is as close in time and possibility as the lady, ringing at the other side of the door—also symbolic of a potential, creative meeting/making of souls?—is near in space and common in our experience. The divinity seems connected somehow to the meeting, the *union*, not simply to be in the lady. In fact it seems that the separate identities of the "lady" and "us" (opening the door) actually merge as the metaphor goes on. The "ringing", like the "buzz" before it, has the quality of an alarm, and this is brought out in the next sentence, suspended pregnantly like the entire paragraph, over dashes—"perhaps that's what alarms" (ll. 7–8). Again there seems to be a link between the idea of the union that is about to take place, the alarm, and the becoming divine. The observation on the progress of her own metaphor, a form of apperception ("perhaps that's what alarms"), discursive thought interrupting visual/metaphorical thought in the overall pattern,[64] also seems to

[64] This level of observation of the thinking/doing self—Coleridge's "Thoughts considered as not I in order to the possibility of the Thought, I—and immediately in order to their possibility as Thoughts considered as I" (*Notebooks*, III, 3575)—seems to me to be in line with his exhortation (regarding the Decalogue): "Not only to obey the pure reason in all our doings & sayings; but

signal a change of direction in it. From being outside the scene, we go inside it, as if we were protagonists, rather like the change in Keats' *Ode on a Grecian Urn* with the stanza "Ah, happy happy boughs! . . ." where Keats seems temporarily to *become,* or to be in 'shared contact' with, his protagonist, the "fair youth beneath the trees" looking up at the sky through the branches representing a change of region and level of perspective on earthly life ("far above"), perhaps in an analogous way to Aeneas' descent into the region of shades (Bk VI) .

So, with "I say I will go myself—" (l. 8), it is as if the bell had rung and we were in the room with her, and she were saying directly: "I'll answer".[65] The "myself", like the elect, seems to say: 'instead of any of you others having the "alarm"' (or the ecstasy—it seems to stand on a knife-edge).[66] At the same time the whole

---

to consider it, of itself, as an object of our care & solicitude—and therefore solemnly to *devote a portion of our time to the principle itself, and the modes of developing, & strengthening our sense of it*—Without this 4th Commandment the 1 & 2nd would become impracticable/ we should soon merge the principle in the outward deeds, & then inevitably the outwards in sensuous motives . . . first merge, & then destroy" (my emphasis). For this seems very much connected to the Romantics' shift of focus of attention from outward, fixed forms, to the "mind"-in-interaction-with-the-object-perceived, as Holmes described so well in Coleridge's pioneering (*Early Visions,* and note 34 above), which may have owed very much to Schiller's work, especially in the period of collaboration with Goethe (see notes 14, 155). It was a shift of attention that Dickinson picked up avidly and learned to wield like her "Giants [did] Himmaleh" (P252). For beautiful elucidation of the progression of this principle in history, through Goethe's effort, see also Stephenson, *Goethe's Conception,* 59–65. For the significance of such change of mode in the technique of construction of the art-symbol, see also Langer, *Philosophy,* in note 149 below.

[65] See, for example, L202: "sitting next evening with Sue, as I often do, someone rang the bell, and I ran, as is my custom", showing the interpenetration of facts of life with the becoming of metaphor.

[66] Compare the idea of the "alarm" with the following passage in L277, showing the poet's task as "assisting the cross": "Perhaps you tire—now—A small weight—is obnoxious—upon a weary rope—but had you Exile—or Eclipse—or so huge a Danger, as would dissolve all other friends—'twould please me to remain—Let others show—this Surry's Grace—/ Myself assist his Cross". (According to Johnson's note Surrey, the first writer of blank verse in English, was tried for high treason before a packed jury and beheaded.) Dickinson seems to be foreseeing the possibility of something like England's

sentence seems also to hold: "I will go on the journey myself" (and be the lady who then rings at the door)—and this is brought out by the images that follow ("I cross the river—and climb the fence—now I am at the gate—Mary—").

The crossing-the-river and so on are, in any case, metaphors of the emotional difficulties and obstacles experienced in preparation for the meeting. But in the working them out, as I said before, the identities of the visitor and recipient seem to merge into the one thing, "it", the event of the meeting/point of contact/relationship;[67] and our divinity seems to consist in this. Similarly, "now I am in the hall" is as if she were both the lady let in after ringing the bell and the house-owner going through the hall to the door to let the lady in to make the meeting possible: "now I am looking your heart in the Eye" (l. 10). So this journey or opening-the-door is one that not only enables you to look somebody in the eye, but to look into the eye of their heart, their deepest core, which is, one imagines, however, where they also see you from most penetratingly; for again there is a strange reciprocity in the expression Dickinson has forged. "I am looking you in the eye" can suggest honesty between people, but it can also suggest defiance and dishonesty, automatic disobedience. The elaboration of the metaphor here usurps the cliché quality of it. So that I look into your heart as if I

"shameful conquest of herself" (*Richard II*): the possibility of each man's or a nation's or the universe's turning against his sun or king and destroying his living principle. The poet's function is to make that present/to be there in its presence/to be present when it happens ("to assist his Cross" is loaded). Let others show his Grace—that is: be the loud applauders of his favoured poetic dexterity on the one hand and on the other his self-righteous murderers. They have the pleasant part (saying nice things), though they are also ironically his death. The poet, like the small weight upon the weary rope (hanging was a current form of capital punishment in Dickinson's time), has the harder part: among those, in a very important sense, who will flatter, then murder Christ (assist the cross—help set it up), he must crucifyingly be aware of the Crucifixion (he cannot pretend Christ is being killed righteously for treason), he must tell the truth (assist the cross—share the suffering, alleviate the pain, bring out the truth). See also her play on the idea of the poet's "myself" bearing things "not of Ourself" (L271, with sources in *John* 14:10 and *Matthew* 10:20).

[67] See, e.g., P448. See also Appendix B: The "Loaded Gun", the "pencil in the hand lightly created", and "it": qualities of creativity. In the context of this issue, see also note 42 above.

see your essence, know you, as in the shade of the faded conventional metaphor. But because it is dislocated from the conventional metaphor, the "Eye" is too much an eye—it sees back as an eye should, in its new context. Not that the metaphor becomes literal, but that we are woken from the sleep of our "film of familiarity" with words,[68] by the alarm of the re-creation of the familiar expression, and perhaps reminded more of the concrete, so that there is an interaction of some sort between the two beings and it is deeply woven into, perhaps even only really created in, the language.

The transition in the next paragraph seems even more difficult. "Did it wait for me—Did it go with the Company? Cruel Company—who have the stocks—and farms—and creeds—and it has just its heart!" Emily Dickinson came to use "it" often for people, and "she" and "he" for things (as in "Summer" later), which may have something to do with Homans' idea of her trying to "move beyond sexual distinctions by creating a gender-free discourse",[69] though it seems to me a more complex phenomenon than this. Emily was "Uncle" and "Aunt", had the "beard" and "petals" (L315 & L233 discussed below). But these were not the only dichotomies with which she experimented within herself: she was also "wife" and "best little girl" (P1072, L248), fast and slow, large and small, for example. I suggest that she uses "it" when she is netting in for speculation an aspect of a person-involved-in-experience, or elements in interaction where it is the *quality* of the emotionality that is defining, and where it is the universal significance of that conjoining experience that counts. For example, the "Representative of the Verse" would be "it" as would the "fraction" in "The Flight of such a fraction takes all our numbers home" (L641)—literally Higginson's newly-dead baby girl. Just before she died, she called her "Friend" Wadsworth "itself a Vision" (L1040), and the "Aborigine of the sky" of the same breath would seem to link the "itself" to the star–immortal soul metaphor that she develops in the late period (see discussion in II.3), as well as it

[68] Coleridge, *Biographia Literaria*, ed. G. Watson, London: Dent, 1975, Ch. XIV, 169.

[69] As Joanne Feit Diehl describes it, in *Dickinson & the Romantic Imagination*, Princeton, NJ: Princeton University Press, 1981, 12n. (henceforth *Dickinson*).

seeming to be linked in the same letter (by "Vision" and "Legend") to the work of art and not accidentally to Keats.[70]

So, in this (1861) letter, the leap from "you" to "it" has to do, not with her being interested in what might be called the social standing of Mary, but with them-in-this-experience-of-meeting and bringing "remembering" closer to "knowing".

It may also help to refer to a passage in the second Master letter (L233) to which this letter is similar:[71]

> I don't know what you can do for it—thank you—Master—but if I had the Beard on my Cheek—like you—and you—had Daisy's petals—and you cared so for me—what would

---

[70] See note 44 above.

[71] I do not use the "Master" letters as primary material in this study for reasons of method. Still, one cannot but help observe the resemblance of these to the broken and emerging language in this 1861 letter, or, for another example, the spring, 1862, L262 to Mrs Bowles: "When the Best is gone—I know that other things are not of consequence—The Heart wants what it wants or else it does not care—. . . I wonder how the love of Christ, is done—when that—below—holds—so—"; "I am older—tonight, Master—but the love is the same—so are the moon and the crescent. If it had been God's will that I might breathe where you breathed—and find the place—myself—at night—if I (can) never forget that I am not with you—and that sorrow and frost are nearer than I . . . the prank of the Heart at play on the Heart—in holy Holiday—is forbidden me—. . . " (L233). Apart from breaking the sentences often, the dashes, or the spaces these create, also give a feeling of large parts of the meaning being contained there, not made explicit, as if she were hewing on a rough block and did not sculpt every link between the parts of the body but left one to surmise them. The parts of language that are there, not elaborated in propositional syntax, are extremely potent as germs of images or longer metaphors: "He built the heart in me—Bye and bye it outgrew me—and like the little mother—with the big child—I got tired holding him—. . . " (L233 again). All these letters seem so haunted by sexual images, images of a pregnant woman, the state of a woman holding, with difficulty, some other life in her that is bursting to come out, that they seem expressive of quite radical reorganization and development. Also see my article, "Representations of the Male in the Female Imagination: The Brontës and Dickinson" (note 21 above) for further discussion of two "Master" letters. The fight–flight–foreign land metaphor may have a source in the story of Moses and also bear some relation to the metaphor of the Emigrant (see Section II.3 and *passim*). The metaphor of the journey to Heaven may owe something to *John* 17:24. She quotes part of this last passage verbatim in the 1851 letter, and her different uses of the story in these two contexts are an example of the development in her use of 'sources'.

> become of you? Could you forget me in fight, or flight—or the foreign land? Could'nt Carlo, and you and I walk in the meadows an hour—and nobody care but the Bobolink—and his—a silver scruple? I used to think when I died—I could see you—so I died as fast as I could—but the "Corporation" are going Heaven too so [Eternity] wont be sequestered—now [at all]—Say I may wait for you—say I need go with no stranger to the to me—untried [country] fold—I waited a long time—Master—but I can wait more— . . . —then I can look at my watch—and if the Day is too far declined—we can take the chances [of] for Heaven—What would you do with me if I came "in white?" Have you the little chest to put the Alive—in? . . .

Here the same questions come up, though with more intensity, as in the letters to all her friends. By this phase, she was no longer demanding a simple kind of relief, but trying to elaborate her own difficulty and response, without interfering with her object's person or being interfered with (connected to her "clandestineness" or dread of "talking of hallowed things aloud"). If you (loved object) were me (the lover), what would your feelings be like and what would assuage them? Trying to fight or to flee, to evade your experience of me by evading/denying me? The image of the "hour together", symbolic of the creative union, comes up then, as it was present in the 1851 letter ("When will the hour be that we shall sit together . . . and the balmiest little breeze stealing in at the window?"), where, however, it was more literal than metaphorical and not worked poetically into other images in the linguistic context at all. In this passage the image ("walk in the meadows") moves on another plane, for use in thought and development in metaphor. It leads into the passage that seems to me an attempt at elaboration of a "possible" (that is, real) relationship to the "Master", the metaphor within which the true form of relationship might be created and contained.

The need she expresses is first described as to "see you" (as against 'forgetting' you and being forgotten, but like the 'knowing' you of the 1861 letter). A possible escape or false solution ("flight" and the "foreign land", recalling *Exodus*) had been in "dying" or "going to Heaven" (perhaps analogous to Moses' striking the rock and demanding the promised land?), becoming divine in the orthodox afterlife, where—she had illuded herself—she could at last "see" him. But then that first, mistaken "dying" would be no good, because the "Corporation were going too", it would not be a viably unique place for that particular creative union.

In the jest with the "Corporation" she seems partly to play with the question of literal death (everybody—corporately and corporeally—ends up dead, and "none I think do there embrace"), and with the orthodox idea of afterlife that her background, with its stocks and creeds and laws and precepts,[72] would have her adopt before she could even "try it".[73]

The solution, then, seems to lie not in attaining corporate "Heaven", where individuals are without individuality, without identities, and so without intimate relationships, which are essentially related to creativity/divinity; rather, it lies in "waiting", as long as necessary, perhaps through the "summers of Hesperides" (P1067), till that journey can really be made to get there. The other, second meeting and going to Heaven in the "Master" letter ("we can take the chances for Heaven. . . . Have you the little chest to put the Alive in?") is as if it were a space for soul-making, for identities, for things that really do live, in life and after death or "departure" (L807) (unlike in the orthodox literal afterlife—only another "creed" and a presumptuous one at that) and has to do with a particular, genuine union capable of creation (not democratic, levelling compromise), here depicted as a mixture of marriage, pregnancy, death, and immortality: one comes in white, the other has the chest to put the Alive in. Since it would be rather difficult if we were to reduce the metaphor to literalness, to tell who is the man and who the woman, it might be just as well to call these figures "it", too. This "chest with the Alive in" is like the grave–box that contains the buried babies whose shadows go "plodding on", the phantoms that will miraculously come back

[72] It seems very likely that she had Emily Brontë's "No coward soul is mine" in mind (published 1846; she possessed a copy: see L299; L813b). See my articles, note 21 above; and: "'Myself' and the 'supposed person': Emily Brontë & Dickinson" in eds. R. Baccolini, C. Comellini & V. Fortunati, *Il Centauro Anglo–Americano*, Bologna, CLUEB (July 1998).

[73] L471.

and haunt her; it is like the haunted house of Art where, as she came to say later, "we are mentally permanent" (L39, L35, L459a, & L555, respectively). It is also linked to the image, earlier in the Master letter,[74] of herself as the "little mother—with the big child" who looks for "Redemption" (the Corporation's Heaven?) and finds that enigmatic "something else"; to the suggestion of the drawer holding the photograph or memory earlier in the 1861 letter; and, I suggest, to the bars/prison/star network of images that I discuss with reference to the third (1875) letter in II.3.

So the elliptical, even obscure, quality of the leap in the third paragraph of the 1861 letter may in fact be a feature of its "candor" (L450); it is the rather loaded question she asks Mary's heart when she sees it and it sees her, and extraneous formalities or inappropriate language would simply handicap her possibility for communication. In this question she seems to be considering different kinds of "going to Heaven" or becoming divine—a false and final or a true and eternal one, a semblance or a reality—perhaps parallel to the "near" and "far" of the preceding paragraph. When she 'knows her' again, here and now in the letter, as it were, the photograph in her chest comes alive, looking her "heart in the Eye"; two alternatives are posed: "Did it wait for me—Did it go with the Company?" The one (parallel to the "say I may wait for you", where the alternation of the persona seems again part of the experimentation of roles and the reciprocal nature of the sender/recipient) seems to present the possibility of a union or journey to a Heaven that creates life; the other to preclude life, to involve a journey that is to a final dying in a tomblike Heaven, where the "company" has the lists of stocks and creeds and property but has no idea any more *by what principle and in what spirit* these were created and so no hope of sustaining their meaningful progression. Here "being divine" is "far off".

The image of the "Cruel Company" (a pun throwing the attack on friendship into relief), like the "Corporation" (L233) and images of the industrial revolution in Emily Brontë's work,[75] is evidence of

---

[74] See note 64 above.

[75] For example, "Julian M. and A. G. Rochelle" (or "The Prisoner" for short), ll. 85–88, in *The Complete Poems of Emily Jane Brontë*, ed. C. W. Hatfield, New York: Columbia University Press, 1941.

her not being so oblivious of events in the external world as was once sustained among critics. While also connected to aspects of her contemporary surroundings that did not command her respect[76]—concern with fixed hierarchy, material wealth, religious precepts, "moral foundations",[77] the "real life" and "matter of fact" (L65) about whose constituents she felt she had to disagree with her cautious father—more specifically it is a criticism of "basic assumption" group—or what Coleridge called "factionist"[78]—opinion as a compromise of thought, and so of the truth, and of such group identity as being an impediment to the building of a particular identity, with particular relationship to things, that can "keep the Alive in" or the "Quick on them" (L268). All this is in antithesis to "it" with "just its heart", which—as she said not so

---

[76] See, for example, Bowles' letter to Austin Dickinson (in *Leyda*, 77): "[I have been] indulging in a sort of disgust at everything & everybody—I guess a good deal as Emily feels".

[77] L619. Henry James (*The Europeans*) in fact has "moral grounds". Dickinson's version is probably combined with the Bible (*John*?).

[78] See, for example, *Notebooks* (III, note 54 above) in 1808–1809 period: 3443, 3551, and especially his (implicit) considerations on the motivating factors in this kind of group relationship: "that Actions are mainly if not exclusively determined by calculations of Hope & Fear & c—This closely connected with the habit of judging of a thing not by our own feelings but by what we believe will be the judgment of others—which being universal must needs annihilate all Judgment—& the habit of referring to notions formed from books for the truth & nature of character and passions found in books, instead of trying them by our experience & actual Observation" (by "Judgment" he evidently means "distinguishing power"). See also Dickinson's L321: "Send no union letters. The soul must go by Death alone, so, it must by life, if it is a soul." This question is obviously contingent to the whole issue of the change in view of the relationship between perceiver and perceived and its expression; to Coleridge's distinction between true and "false" poetry; to Dickinson's investigation of the 'true meeting', the "holy chamber" (L210) that can create "the Alive". Once the perceiver shifts to the premise that there may be no fixed points perceived that are not merely instrumental in a process of further discovery, and besides which, that every viable fixed point susceptible of "truth" is not the result of a mathematical compromise but *creative union* of the parts and therefore more than their sum—more than the "words laid end to end", to use Marianne Moore's term for the art-symbol—then any adhesion to "faction" opinion, or any "assumption" that the component elements in a group have anything that can be called "identity" or that can be other than interrrelationship becomes fatuous—"hypothetical", to use Goethe's term (Stephenson, *Goethe's Conception*, 43).

long after of the "few that have Power to us"—"leave[s] no mode—like Tyrian Dye".[79] But the search (constantly under threat of the "fight/flight to the foreign land"?), to establish "it" "within",[80] may help what is left that is still "creative to create itself".[81]

At this point of elaborating the initial "I wish I knew if you kept me?" she relaxes the tension and obscurity of the images and goes into an apparently simple, easy expression of well-wishing, with pronouns on an ordinary plane and childlike imagery of a Blakean quality, as if some spring of well-being had been released: "I hope you are glad—Mary—no pebble in the Brook—no film on noon—". But it is, in a sense, already too late. All that ease, like Wordsworth's "glory in the flower", has undergone a slight transformation. The subtle change (from, say, "well" or "happy") to "glad" picks up the search to distinguish between different kinds of experience that the letter has so far been engaged in. The state that she wishes Mary is not to be well or content, rich or powerful, but "glad" ("just its heart"). The "pebble in the Brook" that stops the water from flowing paradisiacally smoothly is an image showing possible disturbances in this over-easy or perhaps originally-easy relationship with things, similar to the dust and mosquito earlier. The original sense of "glad" seems to have been "smooth" (*OED*). Her dictionary was the 1828 Webster—smooth, shining, bright, loose, causing joy.[82] And as well as recalling the "river" of the previous paragraph, it links up to the airy, charmlike couplets

---

[79] L275. See also L261: "Can you tell me how to grow—or is it unconveyed—like Melody—or Witchcraft?", where the—characteristic—pressurizing brought to bear on the adjective stretches its significance (unconveyed: unconveyable/without a vehicle-mode).

[80] See her use of this term, for example in L292 (June 1864): "there is a June when Corn is cut, whose option is within", which rings of Milton's "then wilt thou not be loath / To leave this Paradise, but shalt possess / A paradise within thee, happier far" (*P.L.*, XII, 585–587). She called Milton (L1038) the "great florist". I wonder if perhaps her concept of the "waiting" did not owe something to that in Milton's sonnet on his blindness ("They also serve who only stand and wait").

[81] Keats, letter to Hessey, 8 October 1818.

[82] Contrary to the usual assumption that the Dickinson household's was the 1847 edition, see Griffin Wolff (*Emily Dickinson*, note 34 to p. 91).

at the end of the letter. The image of flowing water, in one form or another, was one she often used to express affection streaming towards its object, and flooding water the perilous, overwhelming aspect of these feelings (e.g. L559). "Today" is emphatically and precariously placed between the pebble in the brook and the film on noon, as if on the one hand it exalted the gladness of this day/moment in time at the point in the letter where the tone opens out and seems to suggest the temporary finding of the other person or the relationship where the "Alive" might be. And yet on the other hand it is as if it also threw the shadow of its opposite, saying "today" is one thing but 'yesterday and tomorrow' are different. The "film on noon" recalls the "film of familiarity" in consequence of which we "have eyes yet see not, ears that hear not, and hearts that neither feel nor understand",[83] or perhaps the "film of familiarity which obscures from us the wonder of our Being".[84] These same words and images are reworked in a letter later that year (L245, Dec. 1861):[85]

> Your letter didn't surprise me. . . . I brushed away the sleet from eyes familiar with it—looked again to be sure I read it right—then took up my work hemming strings for mother's gown. I think I bound them faster for knowing you weren't coming. . . .

and this suggests the link for her between film and familiarity (sleet–tears on eyes that do not "see" clearly/that "see" well enough to cry).

So, in the context of the Mary Bowles letter, the film, like the pebble and in contrast to the spirit of "gladness" (linked to "seeing" the "wonder of our Being", and perhaps connected to the visionary "seeing" of the second Master letter), represents the impediment to joy, connected to tears (of sadness) like the "sleet", and also to cynical lack of imagination, life without meaning, over-

---

[83] Coleridge, *Biographia Literaria*, Ch. XIV, after Mark's Gospel.

[84] Shelley, *A Defence of Poetry*, from Coleridge, to go back only one step in the source for this image of the film/veil.

[85] Cf. images in P618; and "sleet" and "snow" images in L432, discussed in Section II.3.

used fixed forms of words not tried "upon our pulses", like the film of familiarity. "Noon" seems representative of the prime moment of something, the sun at its highest; and there again, as throughout the letter, there seems to be the image of seeing God "not through a glass darkly, but face to face" behind the poetic compression of "no film on noon"—that is, no film of tears or familiarity covering your eyes and coming between their clear vision and the bright midday sun (traditionally a representation of Christ). It does not take much to imagine the blinding perilousness inherent in this last image, and I suggest it is linked to the metaphor of the poet as "Emigrant" and searcher for his lost, which we shall see gradually emerging. This also seems to relate to the "flight or the foreign land", which may in one aspect, as said before, represent the false search (basking in the fatuous certainties of orthodox Redemption, for example); but the "fleer–Emigrant" link may also represent an inevitable, though fatal, step in the discovery of the true search. The poet may discover the truth, but he does not save himself by doing so: Moses could envisage, but he never attained, the promised land. "Magic, as it electrifies, also makes decrepit" (L622).

But this mood of ease and innocence, with its shadow before and behind it, continues ("I can think how you look—You cant think how I look", l. 16), and the tone is hide-and-seek playful. It seems to reflect the questions of the earlier part of the letter, but in a lighter vein. "I can think how you look" recalls "I remember you"—though perhaps it would be more vivid now, as if trying to put more energy into the attempt to see whether she can actually 'know' or "see" her if she tries; and so "You cant think how I look" recalls "I wish I knew if you kept me". But she seems able now more freely to attempt a portrait of herself in the absence of being 'known' in her current form. One is reminded of her remarks to Higginson about her distaste for being photographed (L268)—though in fact she seemed to have a fairly contradictory attitude towards it[86]—and for her father's desire to have a "Mold"

[86] She also said her mother looked so beautiful when she was buried that it seemed a "picture" was being "hidden" in the grave (L785).

of her (this word a dig at him and harbinger of her pun on "Quick"), as he did of "all the others"—her reason being that she "noticed the Quick wore off those things, in a few days" and "forestall[s] the dishonor". Her own proposition for overcoming caducity in this area can be seen in the word-portraits she made of herself: the famous "[I] am small, like the Wren, and my Hair is bold, like the chestnut Bur—and my eyes, like the Sherry in the Glass, that the Guest leaves" and this one; and in the context of the search for a form for that "possible" relationship to another being (or being within oneself) that could be creative, keep the "Quick" on it, "keep the Alive in", which is the source of our "glad-ness" and indeed the "wonder of our Being".

After the portrait has been attempted, it is as if a countdown suddenly begins in the move from time-suspended to time being measured with some urgency—"Summer went very fast"—and under this aegis the rest of the letter moves into "minor news" (L521) and furthering the chain of greetings from sender/recipient to other specific intimate ties of theirs, as if moving from general—"it"—to particular: "Emily, Vinnie, Meme, Austin", eternal to transient. And the transition has something of the quality of Marvell's "But at my back I alwaies hear / Time's wingèd chariot hurrying near".

The image of summer as "she" (l. 20), who "got as far as the woman from the Hill—who brings the Blueberry", seems poetically related to the earlier woman-coming-to-the-door-bringing-divinity ("it"), through the connection between blue/royalty/divinity. It must have some affiliation with Calvary and Mary Magdalene's discovery of Christ's resurrection. The description has about it a poignant and slightly dreamy quality quite absent from the subsequent conjuring with "winter" and is reminiscent of "As imperceptibly as grief" (P1540, conjectured 1865), where Summer's departure—not presence—seems to be what creates the "Beautiful", just as indeed here it seems as if the "Blueberry", emblematic of the beautiful, is obtained when summer has gone, where "she" meets she, a long way away, absent but imaginable. The way Dickinson uses "Blueberry" is characteristic of a way she develops of making words 'emblematic', in connection with her enquiry into the relation of word-object/object-word (like the "Can I rely on your 'name'?" later). Such a use of words makes them seem more than simple images, in that it seems they would be a centre of significance even outside their context;[87] and different from symbols in having a less evolved and abstract function, almost as if they were pictures or tokens of even bits of temporizing fancy-dress put on to see whether they might represent the essence of their whole context for a moment, before the decision may be made that 'that is the word that thing is', or the symbol by which it can enter working metaphor permanently.

The jest with "winter"—part of the "minor news" (in summer I did, in winter I will do)—is topical social comment and in fact gives credence to the dating of this letter. Fool-like, it reminds of Hamlet's "I say we will have no moe marriage" (III. i. 149–150),[88] and has a deep and sensible sadness within it ("on account of the soldiers"). The next sentence is pure, bitter irony against the nonsensical activities men become involved in in paralysing states of war ("Since I cannot weave . . . Boots", for as we were later to find out, she only 'wove Books'). The "Memorial", an important "Company" occasion, is perhaps also used as a pun on "memorandum" (also suggested by the elliptical notelike quality of the sentence it comes in: "Shall present . . . "). And thus, "when the Maples turn", when what we habitually call "winter" begins, she will let God know that she wants nothing to do with that "season" (of nonesense). Here again is the suggestion of the "Company" values—it is the Corporation God who is fixing up the war, and to him appropriately she will send a businesslike note—for he wouldn't understand anything else—to explain her adherence to her own "seasons" and to remind him (joggling "Memorial" out of its fixed automatic rut, to re-try it) of the war dead.

---

[87] Cf. Sewall (*Life*, 622) regarding "inasmuch" (L712). Also "since" in L 791. Cf. in this connection, Coleridge in a moment of theorizing what Holmes (*Early Visions*, 281) has termed his new, Romantic "telegraphic" mode of writing, in *Notebooks*, III, 3890: "I am much delighted . . . with the hypothesis . . . that Christ in repeating Eli, Eli, lama sabacthani, really repeated the whole 22nd Psalm . . . To this day to repeat in the same manner but the first line of a common Hymn would be understood as a reference to the whole—".

[88] The "Master" L233, referred to above, is also shadowed by *Hamlet*, for example: "untried country". See also L752 (14 May 1881): "Undiscovered Country"; and P832, P1351.

Dickinson has moved the letter into time in this area, common seasons, as all lovers live with common death before them. But she also seems to have been distinguishing her own inner reality from these, as Keats did in *La Belle Dame Sans Merci*, and Milton before him in "not to me returns / Day, or the sweet approach of even or morn".[89] Summer (traditionally the season that 'stands for' flowering beauty) departs, but in its departure becomes beautiful; winter (traditionally the season of withering) shall not be, instead it is beautified: "when the Maples turn". Turn 'red', of course.

And suddenly, from this context, that strange interjection "Can I rely on your 'name'?" surfaces,[90] recalling the initial direction of enquiry of the letter: she didn't know Mary, but remembered her, had a picture, a sign, a word for her—did this correspond to what Mary was now, particularly in the sense of the token having been exchanged like a pledge ("trawthe"); did Mary still "keep her"? Was the meeting of their souls still possible, as the memory or "name" she had for her suggested it might be? Was the "wile" of this word a barren deceit like the Company Heaven/Memorial and the hope of the hour together with the shutters closed; or part of the creation of what is creative, the "fictitious" that comes of this being "so fair a place"?[91]

It also seems, though, that "Can I rely on your 'name'?" leads in from the distinguishing of her inner seasons from external seasons and their Company "names" that was taking place in the previous paragraph. Similarly, Mary's "garden" that follows would seem to be also "fictitious": that is, an "invisible reality", a metaphor for her inner life, her self, what she is behind the "name", in contradiction or accordance with it, as she perhaps searches for a more adequate

---

[89] *P.L.*, III, 41/42. See her own derivative L790: "sorrow brings its own chill. Seasons do not warm it."

[90] Perhaps with a source in Juliet's speech: "What's in a name ... " (II. ii. 43). To be sure, there is the shadow of her all-pervading metaphor of Jacob wrestling with the angel (*Genesis* 32: 24–32), in the agonistic testing-out of the name-perceived object congruence. In my view, one can see an identical compression of sources, and a typical conjoining of significance, in L720 ("recipient unknown", about 1881): "Let me go for the day breaketh", though Johnson only cites the Bible. See also in this connection, L. A. Willoughby's "'Name' ist Schall und Rauch': On the Significance of Names for Goethe", in *German Life & Letters*, Oxford (April and July 1963), XVI, 3–4, 294–307.

[91] L330: "It is difficult not to be fictitious in so fair a place, but test's severe repairs are permitted all."

one. The Pinks and Sweet Williams seem like internal saints or figures, perhaps pointing up the inadequacy of the name "Mary" in telling her anything about Mary's "heart" in contrast with the explicitness of the flowers' names about certain essential qualities. This questioning of their relationship (are they "true": faithful, committed, alive, real?) is a reflection of the attempt at the 'meeting' between herself and Mary in the earlier part of the letter, which ends in the peculiar word-portrait of Emily.[92]

Then, it seems, she describes her own inner life at that moment of time: "I've got a Geranium like a Sultana—and when the Humming birds come down—Geranium and I shut our eyes—and go far away". It is interesting to note how it contrasts with the first metaphor of her inner state in the letter ("The Dust like the Mosquito . . ."), though it is structurally similar: the sound of "and when the Humming birds come down" contrasts markedly with the "buzz" of the earlier passage, suggesting harmony and ease, and the image seems to suggest the bird coming to suck at the flower. The "Sultana" image seems to suggest, on the one hand, the Eastern purple or white flower ("Sultan"). She writes of this in a later letter (746) in a context of "Geraniums", but also of Presi-

[92] It is interesting to compare the deeply enquiring atmosphere of the letter here—where Dickinson is, as it were, asking "What is your name?", "Who are you?", "What are you?"—to the "Master" L233: "Say I need go with no stranger to the to me untried country". It is as if she were asking that the figure (external or internal) who asks her "what she is" on the day of Judgement should not be a "stranger", should have some knowledge of her, and she of "it". She later worked this idea-feeling, I think, into something partially congruent with Plato's "know thyself" (see, e.g., P832, P1351), though she was never solipsistic—indeed, ever more distant from such a position, the maturer she became, contrary to the myth of her social habits. Her figure of the "stranger" that could totally smash up the creative possibility of the true "going to Heaven" reminds one of Euripides' "Stranger" (Guest–Host) in the *Bacchae* (Dionysus: an Eastern, originally foreign god even to fifth-century Greeks), when he tells Pentheus in the extraordinarily subtle, crucial sticomythia in the central part of the play (c. ll. 461 through 970, with choral variations, etc.) that he does not know "who or what he is" (l. 506), which is essentially related to the fall of his "House". It seems clear, too, that the figure of the "Stranger" is related to the the lady coming to the door. Cf. L752 for an interesting compound of the strange voice/figure-at-the-door/alarm, as Dickinson recounts an external event. See also F. Strich's account of Asian/Christian, 5th-century Greek and Germanic elements in the historical formation of Romanticisim in "Europe and the Romantic Movement" (in *German Life & Letters*, Oxford [January 1949], II, 2, 85–90), such as must have made a deep impact on Dickinson, as on Coleridge before her.

dents, God, "Gardener",[93] and such "Eastern Creatures" (L746). And these, thus (especially in the light of the colouring) may be present in the pun here (which also involves her masquerading as a man: Sultanas lie with Sultans). On the other hand, it suggests the purple bird ("Sultana"). Again, as with the Dido-like "Tyrian Dye", there may be a link between the suggestion of Purple/Eastern kings–gods (merged with Christ risen) and the "Blue" images in the 1861 letter that seem connected to divinity/divine royalty and eternity. And the suggestion of the exotic East (seen again later in the image of Austin in its more Christian aspect), while possibly being an interest that grew out of her involvement with the European Romantic movement, may be connected to the "Emigrant"/ "foreign land" question I have raised before, to the being "far away" from "Home", while simultaneously being in it, and vice versa. The interlocking tension of all these possibilities lead richly into "Geranium and I shut our eyes—and go far away", which also more simply suggests a mother and child wrapped together in rêverie, as if the baby were sucking at the breast (an image transferred from the preceding Humming bird/bee image), or lovers' concentrated absorption. And it may also relate, especially considering the network of images above, to the "shutting our eyes" of the "going to Heaven" of the metaphor of the "possible" relationship to the loved object.

The suggestion seems to be the opposite of the "faith-attacked" of the first metaphor: rather, of complete faith—the child can fearlessly shut its eyes and "go far away", re-find its Home after or through venturing forth, find itself. The "going far away" recalls the "long way" of the fifth paragraph (l. 22); which in turn recalls the "far off" of the second (l. 6), by now in the opposite aspect of meaning, I think, a transformation that seems to me a constant possibility in her metaphor. The fly/mosquito's sting is, if temporarily, held at bay. The eye that pierced with its stare, and was pierced, can be shut, and—again temporarily—accept the "going to Heaven"—where the "celestial Light" (if I came "in white"?) can

[93] Whatever the topical reference in the letter, it seems likely that she connects it to the Shakespearean metaphor of the King/God as Gardener (*Richard II*: III. iv. 159–160). Another source is also perhaps *A Midsummer Night's Dream*: II. i. 165–172. *Antony & Cleopatra* floods all her mature work.

"shine inwards" (into the "chest"–mind?) and allow it to "see and tell / Of things invisible to mortal sight".[94] That is: not stocks, creeds, and properties, but "Life", "the finest Secret", the "Alive". By this stage of the letter, then, the "far away", is that of "absorption" not of "oblivion",[95] and I suggest the beginning of that "feed [ing] on thoughts, that voluntary move / Harmonious numbers" (*P. L.*, III, 37–38), just as it is the "departures" of the "great confidences of Life" that disclose them, after which we "dream of [them], and sing of [them] and paint [them]" (L379). The "communion with the spirits of our love" that is exterior to time has, as it were, found a transitional form.

The circle then widens again, from the description of the internal garden to close external figures seen experimentally in a particular aspect. The greeting to Mary as "Meme" (a pun on "Me–me" in the context of the making of identity, rather like Blake's "Lyca"/ "like her" in *The Little Girl Lost* and *Found*) picks up the themes and images of the rest of the letter. The offer of vitalizing love in the offer of the "Butterfly" (a re-domesticated version of the god of the soul, spirit, breath, 'Psyche' and possibly a pun on "better—fly", "with a vest like a Turk" linking to the Eastern images and suggesting combativeness) seems similar to the lady bringing the Blueberry, or the lady ringing at the door of the house. It seems as if the change in the course of the letter from fear, distrust, uncertainty to a certain ease and self-confidence is expressed in the mosquito/fly becoming the "Butter-fly" and the latent "blue-buzz" becoming the "Blue-berry" and "Blue Sea". The conditional clause "if she will build him a House in her 'Morning-Glory'" (II, 31–32), which is certainly bartering and perhaps latently mistrustful in mood, seems an analogous request or proviso that there be a reciprocator or responding container, to that in her image elsewhere of a person with the "chest to put the Alive in" and of the "haunted House" of art. "Morning-Glory" seems a pun on the name of the blue flower,

[94] *P.L.*, III, 51–55. I believe there is a derivative relation between her metaphor of the "verse that breathes" that is ramified vastly throughout her work, and Milton's "Light shining inwards" metaphor.

[95] L342b, in Higginson's letter relating statements by Dickinson: "Is it absorption or oblivion when things pass from our minds?", Ruth Miller (*Miller*, 423–426) reprints in her Appendix III on "Emily Dickinson's Reading" a section on "Oblivion" by Sir Thomas Browne, from Chambers' *Cyclopaedia of English Literature: A Selection of the Choicest Productions of English Authors from the Earliest to the Present Time*, 1847, which was in the Dickinson library.

referring to Mamie's age and tapping the "Immortality Ode", but it also has some reference to Mary Magdalene's discovery of the 'victory' of the resurrection (after 'Mourning') and is part of the newly evident militant metaphor. And the presence of the flower image also recalls the image of the butterfly/bee/Humming bird going to suck, and thus all the images this was related to and the exploratory significance they carry.

The end of the last paragraph consists in little cameos of her sister, mother, and brother. They have a slight quality of disappointment about them—"they would send their love *but*"—as if she felt in some way forsaken or let down by them ("I bring my own—myself"). And one wonders why her father is not among the named—perhaps "too intrinsic" (P1393) to her? But as she herself indirectly suggests throughout the whole letter in the "knowing–remembering" theme, these represent her feelings about them, her picture of them—more specifically, them in the context of this letter, these metaphors being elaborated, this poetic language. They are not them in fact. And in this sense they are as much internal figures as the earlier landscape was mental.

For example, the picture of Vinnie ("but she put on a white frock, and went to meet tomorrow") is strikingly close to her picture of herself in the "Master" letter discussed earlier: "What would you do with me if I came 'in white'? Have you the little chest to put the Alive in?" It is jocular as well as earnest in a way that the Master letter really is not. Her game with the "names" of "time" in "went to meet tomorrow—a few minutes ago" is fundamentally a serious experiment analogous to the "far off/near", "Summer went a long way very fast/winter will not be" experiments of before, in the nature of 'where does meaning lie?'; 'can you really deduce reality from appearances?'; 'in what sense *is* meaning reality, for the human being?'[96] One sees this progres-

[96] In this area, her investigation was very much in line with Coleridge's: see, for example, his *Notebooks*, III, 4058: "Is it then nothing, to have *intelligibly* generated the main agents in all the Phaenomena of observable Nature, instead of assuming them as a somewhat common to the several classes, . . . you know that the moon's real motion and its apparent are two different things, the latter of which only can be determined by mere observation.. . . That, should you say, the former is deduced from it, you could attach no meaning to the word deduced . . . And you cannot but smile at the position, that the certainty of the moon's real motion is derived from a deceptive appearance, which ceases to be

sively being played out in her relation of tenses and moods, too. The force of these games with words and their syntactical relations as containers of "some thing" make internal reality (Truth) and external reality (Fact) clash against each other in a dynamic and significant way: things are only what they seem, yet what they seem is not necessarily how they are. "Count not that far that can be had / Though sunset lie between—/ Nor that adjacent, that beside. / Is further than the sun." (L318). Analogously we are both interior and exterior to time and space, the very concepts of whose 'reality' she throws into question.

Again, the picture of her mother seems to me to bear a similar relation to her. Here the characterization gives us a tiny person in an out-of-the-way place (in the "eave-spout"—it sounds even more desperate than poor Troilus, who "thorugh a goter, by a pryve wente"[97] to engage the love of his life), totally caught up in an apparently finnicky and futile task (sweeping up one leaf of all the leaves that fall, and *that* of the year before), and so obsessed with cleaning out the potential channel for the flood of her affection that she omits to allow any to actually be generated. And yet the picture is reminiscent of an aspect of Dickinson's own view of herself. She is small like the Wren (small enough to get into an eavespout), she "tills" the ground in search of "vanished bulbs" (friends);[98] time is nothing of significance in the realm of meaning—"Long years apart—can make no / Breach a second cannot fill—" (P1383), last year's leaf is as significant as this year's; and "*a* leaf"—well, is not "each a World?" (L890). Other remarks of a similar cruelty also ring of her own make-up—for example: "Mother is much as usual. I know not what to hope for her" (L191).[99] Or else (actually of her mother's "favourite sister" during a serious illness, but it might as

---

deceptive then first, when it is deduced from the real motion—according to what law? And from what has the real motion of the Moon, itself, deduced? And what is the object of such deduction? Is it not, *first* intelligibility—in order to understand the appearances—and second, the power of Prophecy independent of past experience . . . etc . . . ".

[97] Chaucer, *Troilus & Criseyde*, III, 787.

[98] L824: "Is not an absent friend as mysterious as a bulb in the ground, and is not a bulb the most captivating floral form?"; and L207 for "tilling".

[99] Written probably about the period when she was beginning to realize the cost of becoming a poet and working with that "seed of disappointment / Within a capsule gay" (L390). See also how: "Sermons on unbelief ever did

well have been about her mother): "Does God take care of those at sea? My aunt is such a timid woman!".[100]

And while her mother's desertion seems to consist in doing too little, her brother's consists in doing too much: "he married—and went East." "East" refers partly to the resurrection/Sun rising, like the summer that departs "into the Beautiful"; as well as to all the images of the East discussed before. It is also perhaps a piece of topical irony on the fact that Austin had planned to move west when he married, like so many people at that time, but ended up in the house next-door (East—opposite to moving far—West), where paradoxically in himself he seemed to become more distant than ever, like the risen sun. As she said of him and of her father (L432, the basis of Section II.3 below): "We missed him while he was with us and we missed him when he was gone", which, like everything else compounded by our self-confessed "ardent liar" (L315), is not to be taken at face value.

Like Chaucer's miniatures of Criseyde, Troilus, and Diomede towards the end of his romance (V, 806–840), these rather statuesque, though slightly caricatured little pictures have something of a 'goodbye' about them. Perhaps the sense of loss of her external family is no accident in view of the thrust in the rest of the letter to create a space for the rebirth and even re-formation of feeling and relationship to things, and to find the right language—'reliable

---

attract me" (L176), and: "the loveliest sermon I ever heard was the disappointment of Jesus in Judas" (L385). Cf also L472: "We thank thee Oh Father for these strange Minds, that enamor us against thee", expressing something of the "elastic ratio" (L683) between self and object in which her "Gymnastic Destiny" (L685) involved her. Judas-the-betrayer and Jesus-the-forgiver seem related to the ambiguous "Emigrant" figure mentioned before—contrasting aspects between which the man-becoming-poet moves as he searches for the truth. Topically, and historically, the "Emigrant" image probably has some link to the emigrés of the French Revolution and their vicissitudes.

[100] L207. A telling incident that touches on this, though of a later date, occurs in L687: "I ask Mother 'what message' she sends—She says, 'Tell them I wish I could take them both in my Arms and carry them—' I never before have heard her speak so—those were the very words—", where Dickinson is evidently surprised to hear her mother sound 'just like herself' (see Letter 50, ll. 85–86)! A revelation of the sort, I think, begs the question as to who is the forgiver and who the betrayer, to relate it to the Jesus–Judas problem mentioned above.

names', as it were, in which these may find some expression, on a different basis from that of the past. It is certainly tempting to trace some link between the search for the true, eye-to-eye-of-the-heart relationship with Mary (Me–me) and the nature of her own internal relationships through the deeply compressed and extraordinary language (that branches back into the past and, as we shall see, into the future), and the contrasting rejection of the "Company" values and what seems here a rather out-dated, fossilized picture of her factual family. It is as if she were trying, in the very language and form of the letter, to transform these old images, linked to a perhaps more externally dependent relationship to the object of her vision and always an "option" anyway ("Did it go with the Company?"), by trying to repaint them in view of the the "Light shining inwards" or words that come from a chest that really breathes, to repaint the 'truth' about herself, and then herself-in-relation-to-them (seen in the metaphors of the true meeting and "Geranium and I"?). So that the language she finds to describe her relationships really is beginning to tell "of things invisible to mortal sight", to conceive invisible realities, to be that toilsome yet "unpremeditated" thing,[101] 'poetic'.

These two paradoxical aspects of the poetic experience—the work she experiences as her own and that she experiences as inspired (the one more like drudgery and the other more like danger or "alarm"—perhaps akin to the distinction Dickinson makes elsewhere between "Labor" and "Action"),[102] seem beautifully held in two mirror sentences: "I brought my own—myself"; "I could not weigh myself—myself" (L261). And in the letter the first of these picks up the "I say I will go myself" of the lady-at-the-door metaphor, thus connecting divinity, love, and making the "Alive" (a child, a flower, a verse that breathes). And the letter ends, in one sense resolved, in a bold exhortation: "please remember me" (instead of the despairing "I wish I knew if you kept me"), and a statement of ecstatic faith: "I remember you—Always" (rather than the faltering "several times" in a "long while"), and the uninhibited flow of the spiritlike—again rather Blakean—couplets.

---

[101] *P.L.*, III, 55; IX, 24, respectively.

[102] L459: "Labor might fatigue, though it is Action's Rest".

These once more pick up the themes and images that are woven through the letter, and particularly the "glad" section: the river flowing, the blue sea (linked to the "Blueberry"); and "I'll fetch thee Brooks / . . . nooks" seems to ring of the fairy chant in *A Midsummer Night's Dream* (II. ii. 9–24), warding off evil, as she is warding off untruth and the disintegration of the struggle for the 'meeting' (both internal and external) that can create the "Alive", as if she were indeed dealing with a kind of "magic".[103]

It is worth noting how the last part of this letter (strictly the 'poem' and as such abstracted into Johnson's edition of the *Poems* (P162, conjectured c.1860), is in fact less poetically dynamic than the prose of the rest of the letter. It does less 'making' work on the language and on the thought, and as such, alone, it is less the true descendant of the great poetic tradition it comes from and less the ancestor of whatever lives after. "The stars are not hereditary" (L827). The thinness and oversmoothness of the verse-poem suggests that in the context of the letter it was more intended as a sign-emblem than as 'poetic' work in itself, in the sense that those in the Romantic movement, who really shifted thought forward, considered it: Coleridge, for example, in his *Shakespearean Criticism*,[104] or Shelley in the *Defence*;[105] and, indeed, in the sense that

---

[103] She often saw her work within the metaphor of "magic" and related images. See, for example, L622 and L562; and P1383, where "spell" denotes the magnetism (always treated with a dose of ascetic enquiring) of the binding affection in a relationship, which for her was deeply connected to her experience as a poet and Section II.3, for "spell of Steel".

[104] See, for example, his description of: "a middle state of mind more strictly appropriate to the imagination than any other, when it is, as it were, hovering between images. As soon as it is fixed on one image, it becomes understanding; but while it is unfixed and wavering between them, attaching itself permanently to none, it is imagination" (ed. T. M. Raysor, London: Dent, vol. II, 103).

[105] See, for example: "the popular division into prose and verse is inadmissible in accurate philosophy. . . . it is by no means essential that a poet should accommodate his language to this traditional form, so that the harmony, which

Dickinson, after them, came to consider it. And that is, where it is the showing-through of the *principle* of the materials-in-formation that constitutes the power and interest, the moving aesthetic quality, of the object.

The development of language we have seen at work in this letter, then, is vastly different from the letter of ten years before, though the earlier letter contained some of the same elements: working with quotations and stories/images from the Bible and various authors; stretching words to the circumference of their meanings and usurping their ordinary syntactical collocations, the conventional logical relations of these; movement between different modes of language in showing conjunctions of feeling and thought, and so on. Here I have shown, I hope, that the letter begins to have poetic form, in the sense that the writer's meaning is sought, elaborated, and sustained by metaphors that interweave throughout the letter and lead on to later work. If the couplet-poem at the end does not stand alone poetically, it certainly serves to tie the ends together like the flower or pie (L629) or pencil that Dickinson would enclose with her letters as an emblem of their significance. The metaphors and references related to the Bible and other works are more deeply integrated into the fabric of her own words and more originally used; and she seems to begin to create metaphors and even emblematic words of her own (Juneating, Blueberry, tanned, etc.), rather than to borrow in passive or manipulative imitation. The language is visibly in evolution: elliptical (even too elliptical), full of potential, beginning to really tap and interlock with the rich source of the language system as a whole. And as such, the images and metaphors refer to a network of work beyond this letter, they are part of the "Tree broadening out of sight" (L951). Even the way the letter opens and closes suggests a firmly established capacity to make immediate contact with her

---

is its spirit, be observed . . . All the authors of revolutions in opinion are not only necessarily poets as they are inventors, nor even as their words unveil the permanent analogy of things by images which participate in the life of truth; but as their periods are harmonious and rhythmical, and contain in themselves the elements of verse; being the echo of the eternal music" (*Shelley's Prose*, 275–297).

object and to be recognized in her particularity (the theme of uncertainty merely proves the authenticity of her knowledge of the process required to earn such intimacy). Her use of individual words, as of images and metaphors, breaks their familiar or discursively logical boundaries all the time (the Dust buzzing, the eye of the Heart, true flowers, and so on), creating new or re-finding lost dimensions for words and objects as these interact and change one another. And this in a much more emphatic way than before, so that the sense of confusion of these intense states has changed into a sense of significant pressure on the words—images, syntax, concepts—as if on diamond ore, and as if she were creating what she called in another context "a change of heart—though I dont mean a Revolution" (L678). Analogously, the prescriptive grammarian's grammar has shown its relativity, and the punctuation become more particular: the dashes begin to have structuring power, rather like molecular links. In this way, she shakes up our certainties and dormant assumptions, yet "assists" our pain (L277);[106] opens our eyes to connections between ordinary and sublime things in our outside and inside worlds (opening a door, flowers, birds, death, resurrection), while filling these with meaning, and to the "possibility" of forms language, not as alienated from but dynamic to our lives. Not for nothing does one of the key words in the final letter have its source in the Biblical "Behold, I shew you a mystery" (I *Corinthians* 15:51).

This letter is overall more economical, less splashy, more formal; there is a richness of registers in the language: sacred and ritualistic, homely familiar, more humour and more sense of tragedy, in contrast to the earlier letter's long-drawn-out monotone. Ironically while there is great restraint, there is a giddy sense of the possibility of things—connected to the discovery of meaning in the language. It has less of a "breeches pocket" aim,[107] and is more simply observant of how its own destiny will work itself out. There seems to be an observer's eye within the writing monitoring the development of the metaphors being made ("perhaps that's what

---

[106] See above note 65. See also L362: "No part of mind is permanent. This startles the happy, but it assists the sad".

[107] Keats , letter to Reynolds, 3 February 1818.

alarms") as they reach for the "truth" about the life they are describing; as if Dickinson were partly the protagonist of her life in the words, partly the observer of her own "Action", also as poet. And the creation of this space or distinction seems to me connected to the emergence of the "light shining inwards" aspect of the "shutting our eyes and going far away"; finding a vocabulary and network of metaphors enabling her to live and discover real meaning in the world, to reach from the "Centre" to the "Circumference" of possibility. The letter seems to distinguish between internal ("where the meanings are", P258) and external, and with this between what is interior and what exterior to time; where "immortality" can be and where it cannot, and how these opposites are so essential to one another. And herewith are the great themes emerging: the world's great beauty that is apprehended in the possibility of missing it ("You can't think how I look. . . . I hope you are glad") on the one hand, but more so in the certainty of losing it ("Summer went very fast") on the other; the sacredness of the pain (winter beautified in "when the Maples turn") caused by this apprehension in the sense of its direct relation to the search to establish the immortality of beauty ("I remember you—Always") by seeking to be worthy of it in all the forms in which it has been revealed, particularly—though not only—in the closest human forms. Add to that, by seeking to be true to it ("Memorial"), which implies truth to one's self first (the Geranium/Sultana image), and you can include all ill and all humanity. "Sometimes with the Heart, / Seldom with the Soul / Scarcer once with the Might / Few—love at all" (P1680: no date conjectured). And last but not least, as the "little Tippler" (p. 214) would tell us, the sacredness of ecstasy, for the same reasons.

3. Making revolution constant

'It is finished' can never be said of us.

L555, to Mrs. Holland, June 1878
[quoting *John* 19: 30]

LETTER 432, JANUARY 1875, TO MRS HOLLAND

Sister.

This austere Afternoon is more becoming to a Patriot than to one whose Friend is it's sole Land.

No event of Wind or Bird breaks the Spell of Steel.

Nature squanders Rigor—now—where she squandered Love.

Chastening—it may be—the Lass that she receiveth.

My House is a House of Snow—true—sadly—of few.

Mother is asleep in the Library—Vinnie—in the Dining Room—Father—in the Masked Bed—in the marl House.

How soft his Prison is—
How sweet those sullen Bars—
No Despot—but the King of Down
Invented that Repose!

When I think of his firm Light—quenched so causelessly, it fritters the worth of much that shines. "Dust unto the Dust" indeed—but the final clause of that marvelous sentence—who has rendered it?

"I say unto you," Father would read at Prayers, with a militant Accent that would startle one.

Forgive me if I linger on the first Mystery of the House.

It's specific Mystery—each Heart had before—but within this World. Father's was the first Act distinctly of the Spirit.

Austin's Family went to Geneva, and Austin lived with us four weeks. It seemed peculiar—pathetic—and Antediluvian. We missed him while he was with us and missed him when he was gone.

All is so very curious.

Thank you for that "New Year"—the first with a fracture. I trust it is whole and hale—to you.

"Kingsley" rejoins "Argemone"—

Thank you for the Affection. It helps me up the Stairs at Night, where as I passed my Father's Door—I used to think was safety. The Hand that plucked the Clover—I seek, and am

Emily.

[Johnson's note has: Mrs Holland had plucked a spray of clover from Edward Dickinson's grave, which Emily Dickinson never visited, and gave it to her. Argemone is the heroine of Kingsley's first novel, *Yeast*. Kingsley died on 23 January 1875.]

So: to the last letter, written six months after her father's death in June 1874, and still eleven years before her last work and her death in May 1886.

As in the second letter, the plain vocative of the address suggests its unswerving directness, though the generic title substituting the colour of a name adds a sense of austere fellowship. Probably her dearest woman friend and the recipient of some of the most beautiful letters Emily Dickinson left behind, Mrs Holland was addressed by her as "Sister" as far back as 1859, at first—as if it were one of those 'emblematic' words of the 1861 letter, a mask in formation before fully assuming identity with its wearer—in inverted commas, later consistently without.

In fact the "austere" of the opening sentence seems to be a major theme of this letter, perhaps giving way only to the theme of "Mystery" later. Supremely composed, and compressed even to severity—the words fall into place without apology or hesitation and link to an ever-broadening network of metaphor in her broadening thought—it is loaded with intense ambiguities[108] and has overcome the fragmenting ellipsis of the earlier (1861) letter.

---

[108] William Empson's (provisional) categories of ambiguity may be helpful as a starting point here: for example, the fourth or, in particular the seventh, types (*Seven Types of Ambiguity*, Harmondsworth: Penguin [1930] 1961, 192): "[this last] occurs when the two meanings of the word, the two values of the ambiguity, are the two opposite meanings defined by the context, so that the total effect is to show a fundamental division in the writer's mind". The evolution of the model of the mind in studies in psychology and psychoanalysis since then—as indeed I. A. Richards speculated in *Practical Criticsm* (London: Routledge and Kegan Paul [1929] 1978)—probably enables us now to entertain a more complex idea than that of a "division" in the mind, where the art-symbol and the quality of emotionality and thought it presents is concerned.

Initially she seems to be characterizing the external weather: cold and rigidly unwelcoming—austere—typical of the New England winter. But the words quickly hang more heavily: a description of a severe state of things and her own state of mind austerely in a lock with it, attempting to distinguish itself from outside weather and outside events (her father's death) and yet perhaps reshaping itself through the experience of these. What is in "austere" anyway? Beauty? Ugliness, rigorousness and truth, death and rigor mortis? A word we usually use to describe a person's (not an afternoon's) nature, or some habit of a person that indicates the sincerity of their nature, with the "more becoming" that follows, it seems to transform the literal "Afternoon" into a gown or uniform or a gesture or condition that we might consent to put on or take up or be in (like "this trinket of Life we put on", L385, L438), as if it were truly representative of our selves; or else that Nature (personified soon after) puts on as she stands before us in judgement. One thinks of other contexts of the "Afternoon" without its literal dimension as the moment, after the peak of the noonday sun, slipping towards the evenings/reckonings of our lives, the beginning of the soul's loneliness and "bodilessness" (P524), the instigator of "Heavenly Hurt" and "internal difference" (P258).

So one might imagine this "austere Afternoon" as the officialdom of a judge's gown to be put on, a period of hard reckoning to be gone through, a period of trial. And this might be linked on the one hand to the deadly literalness and spiritlessness of the "Patriot" (that follows); but also possibly to the "light escaping / Into the Beautiful" recalled both in the 1861 letter and in a more recent one she wrote immediately after her father's death (L418), and continued in subsequent years in the network of the light/summer/star images, some of which we have seen before and all of which I shall discuss later. I suggest it is also linked poetically to the image of "going up the Stairs at Night" later in this letter.

Her apparent distaste for this dress (it's "more becoming to a Patriot") begins her distinguishing of her self from the condition she finds herself in, her Fate, and throws a hostile light on the equivocal quality of "austere", making it seem purely brutal and frigid and less the "Heavenly Hurt" that is creative of "internal difference". And yet ironically she seems to absorb part of that state of austerity into her 'self' in the form of words she uses to demonstrate her resistance: she would be "gay" but the afternoon is "austere", and she deals with it austerely, becoming austere. "God is penurious with me, which makes me shrewd with him" (L207).

The sense of her own austerity is sown in her courteously firm dismissal of God's creation (the austere Afternoon), played upon our pulses by the semi-alliteration of the phrase and borne out by the dull but insistent monosyllabic thumping of the second half of the sentence: "whose Friend is it's sole Land". This recalls Keats' "To toll me back from thee to my sole self". The Patriot from whom she dissociates herself (as she dismissed the war, for example, in the 1861 letter) seems to me in this context another of those "Company" figures, and this would be borne out by the predominantly hostile aspect of the suggestion of judgement or the judge's robe (giving a man a Company posture rather than an identity, a shell rather than a "kernel") earlier in the sentence.

Here, too, as in the 1861 letter where there are two Heavens distinguished, there seem to be two "Lands" woven directly into the same metaphor, two austerities, even two patriots, that show each other in their opposition, and thus also possibly show how difficult they are to tell apart, and like the rise and fall of the "Flood" (L415), how intrinsically bound the one is to the other's movements. For she ("one") of necessity in the words accepts the metaphor of the "Land" in the same breath as the "Patriot" does, but re-searching it, re-defining it, re-filling it, showing what it is not and what it is (a "friend"—another metaphor or "fiction"?), with perhaps the writer creating, as it were, a third dimension as he looks on and works over the problem. Again, Dickinson makes the group–individual contrast, as she had come to do by the 1861 letter. The Patriot's Land is the Company, the Nation, a generalized idea of a homogenized mass of people, a number, and he relates to the group as such, even brutalizing himself. His judgement knows nothing of a real person, of that "sensible warm motion" whose loss is so deeply felt in this letter, and in a sense compromises his knowledge of 'truth' in his compromise of his relationship to his object; just as the "old fantastical Duke of dark corners" (*Measure for Measure*, IV. iii. 1159–1160) would save a child, but the straight and punctual Duke hypocritically touching up the image of his "apeing" authority would have cost Claudio his life and left a child fatherless, if life had not erupted and overcome his arid schematicness.[109] The other "one's" land, as it were a "little Region to wander in",[110] is a 'real' human being, though "this also is fiction" (L969) and arguably a less generic 'idea-of-a-person'. But at least "one" is potentially less obliged to compromise the vision of the emotional complexity and the sincerity of the relationship, to judge partially and therefore to misjudge himself and his object. The antithesis between the "Patriot" with the capital "P" and the "one" of no status with the small "o" seems to be connected to this and also links to her metaphor of the "barefoot Heart/one/Rank" elsewhere (e.g. L265, L671, L966), and to her antithesis of the "committee" and the individual (L321, L342).

On a perhaps simpler level of abstraction, this first sentence is of course a metaphor, saying that she desperately misses her father. Consider, for example, how she seems to connect her father—as a sole Land or little Region to wander in—to his house/grounds, in comments like: "I do not cross my Father's ground to any House or town" (L330). This regards both her metaphor and her life which seemed to become increasingly integrated—she became more like her poems, her poems became more her. One thinks, for example, of her remark "I thought being a Poem oneself precluded the writing Poems, but perceive the mistake" (L413),[111] a turn of phrase she certainly elaborated from Milton, like her "Book is only the Heart's Portrait—every Page a Pulse" (L794.

---

[109] *Measure for Measure,* IV. iii. 1159–1160 and II. ii. 117–123, respectively. Isabella's is a talented and powerful speech; but her story is an example of the dangers of "writing a Poem" without "being a Poem" (L413), and this is a theme right at the heart of Emily Dickinson's search for the "chiefest words" and the 'true meeting'.

[110] Keats, letter to Bailey, 8 October 1817.

[111] To Higginson. I suspect she never thought any such thing, definitively. Such a statement forms part of her discourse of opposites. Here it is a form of courtesy. It may be very tongue-in-cheek (as I think the Patriot-intellect-Native Land question later in the same letter is), and indeed the problem of irony is extremely difficult to gauge. In particular Austin is supposed to have told Mabel Loomis Todd that "Emily definitely posed in those letters [to Higginson]", and she claimed that Austin knew his sister "thoroughly, through and through, as no one else ever did" (M. L. Todd's journal, quoted in Sewall, *Life,* 538).

Milton: *Areopagitica*). And this connection would illuminate the link between the "Friend" and this kind of "Land" in the metaphor we are dealing with here. But one of the insoluble particles in this statement for any student of Dickinson is how she seems to have set herself against aspects we recognize as part of her: austere (at least socially, and also with herself; it may also be a pun on the name of her deeply loved and apparently painfully contradictory brother); exclusive lover of her own "Land"—a patriot—in the sense that it seems her land came to symbolize her father–friend and the bodiless relationship "where the meanings are", just as that bodiless relationship and little Region to wander in came to move and show that internal journeying and knowledge of herself that she wrought in words.

This metaphorical relationship between land/father–friend/ internal self can be seen working in other comments of a similarly gnomic, Blakean quality. For example: "You noticed my dwelling alone—To an Emigrant, Country is idle except it be his own",[112] where the "Country" links to our "Land" and to "friend" ("his own") and inner self; all the more to this last since the person/poet is an "Emigrant" and therefore only mentally in contact with the absent friend within. Or: "To shut our eyes is Travel" (L354), where the translation of the external to the internal country to be travelled through is made more specific by the shut eyes; and this also relates to the Geranium image of the 1861 letter and, I suggested, the finding of the internal guiding light that illuminates (as the breath of the "wind" brings alive) the internal world (chest–mind/heart) and through which new relationship to the world might be truly sought. It seems she has chosen words that make a confrontation with this paradox inescapable and, as often, throw up the relative inadequacy of words with fixed meanings to describe or explore any complex, vital state, and with this, the enigmaticness or "clandestineness" of words in a poetic context that is capturing "truth".[113] Here their "meaning" is as hard to

---

[112] L330. See other possible links to this metaphor with reference to her enquiry into the nature of the poet in the images of "flight and foreign land", and Jesus–Judas, mentioned in Section II.2.

[113] Compare to her jestingly earnest love of thieves, liars, rogues, and treason: L315, L359, L746 & L851, for example.

explain or unravel as the meaning of the experiences they capture, though it may be felt, intuited, loved, hated, and mistaken many times before its infrastructure is understood. In this letter, similarly, it is misleading to endow "austere" only with a pejorative sense (the shallowness of the Patriot, the numbness of her state); it is misleading to endow it only with the opposite (rigorousness of the seed of knowledge); and yet we lie if we say no distinction is being made between these different aspects, that they are just confused and neither one nor the other. It seems to contain all in a "mob" (L265) battling with each other in relation to the rest of the metaphor (the Company–Patriot is austere and deadly, the barefoot "one whose Friend is its sole Land" becomes austere by its loss and this austerity may have something to do with discovering the truth), and I think to the progress of the letter as it moves from austerity to mystery.

Under the weight of this slightly oracular-sounding statement, the words go into a kind of chant as if demonstrating the absolute mastery of the austerity. The next four lines (ll. 4–8) scan, as if they would break into quatrains of alternate four- and three-stress lines, with a potential rhyme scheme that interlaces, 'birdlike', thus:

—Bird	a
—Steel	a
—now	b
—Love	b
—be	a
—eth	a
—Snow	b
—few	b

The last two lines loosen the rigorousness of the sound of the first two, as if some dissolution were taking place. But, unlike the short, buoyant form of the imminent and sweeter image of her dead father, the heavy impeded long-ness of these lines seems to strengthen the terrible implacability of the spell she is held in. Equally, the sudden end of each long sentence in a self-containing full stop—even where the grammatical sense would spill over—seems doubly abrupt and guillotine-like.

The first chant opens forcefully with "No", creating the barrier it expresses; then the combination of words—"event" as the main noun and "Wind" and "Bird" as genitives—is peculiarly characteristic of Dickinson and has wide reference in the metaphorical context of her writing. "Event" has a sacramental and concrete quality to it in the context, as if it meant the Resurrection or the Apocalypse, and it is strangely raised to more concreteness or importance than the specific earthly forms "wind" and "bird", which, however, take on a kind of spiritual quality in their genitive forms here. None of these words, as I have said, were strangers to her hands by this stage, but have rather particular faces in the network of her metaphor. Closely linked (evidently, as they can almost substitute each other here), they tend to symbolize things in the area of what is poignantly and aetherially beautiful in particular but ephemeral earthly form: fragile and fleeting, yet mighty movers of eternal things. In her earlier letters (including the 1851 one), we witness the almost clichéd "bird flown" returning time and again, passing through the recollection of Keats' nightingale. Later in her letters the image of the "Bird" seems to be recuperated without the catch-phrase as such, as indeed here it is evidently a potentially powerful "event" but often a source of alarm, as the form in which the souls of her friends will depart. And while the "Bird" with its song (one of her images of the poet) seems to represent largely the visual and aural expression of divine beauty in particular form (e.g. L455, L457), the wind, like the breath of God and the Platonic word that in itself imaged inspiration,[114] and indeed like her own "verse that breathes", seems to represent the prime mover of immortal beauty: perhaps like Blake's "gentle wind",[115] it moves "silently and invisibly" but pervades all things and is the link between the earthly form and its divine interlocutor. Naturally enough, both come imaged with ambivalent qualities (e.g. L442, L472).

In this particular context, then, the soft semi-assonance of the "Wind or Bird" crushed mid-sentence evokes a ghostly ethereal quality in earthly beauty. This overturns in the second half of the sentence with the precise and spitefully hard alliteration of "Bird / breaks the spell of Steel" (Bird and Steel also being the only end

[114] *Symposium*: "empneo", to breathe into. Cf also (GK.) "psuchein": to breathe, obviously related to "Psyche", Eros's lover, imaged as a butterfly in mythology. The butterfly–bird link hardly needs comment.

[115] "Never seek to tell thy love".

words with no shadow of a rhyme between them in the scheme, if it has any validity). So the opposing qualities of the two things are evoked: the Bird and Wind, the spell of Steel, as is the negation of the former by the latter, both in the logical sense and in the structure of the sentence. The "spell of Steel" clearly picks up the "austerity" in its hard, rigid aspect, though the "spell" may also have its ambivalent quality in the same way as the austerity, land, and as, indeed, I believe, nearly all her major words do.[116] In fact, the more one looks at her progressing work, the more it seems that she increasingly used words, not in the fixed way Coleridge feared would lead to the degeneration of meaning, but *in themselves* as if they *were* 'things-hovering-between-images'. As soon as you (rationally) shift the emphasis of meaning in the major words in a syntagm, you change vertex on the overall meaning completely,

---

[116] Take the way she thought of her poetic work as "magic", witchcraft, in the sense of its great power to move, to experiment, and to reach for "Circumference", and its irreducibility. This may be inversely related to the question of the Patriot's "Intellect" being his "Native Land" as well (L413), in contrast with her statement elsewhere that "genius is the ignition of affection—not intellect, as is suppposed,—the exaltation of devotion, and in proportion to our capacity for that, is our experience of genius" (L691). That is, the power whose grip she is in is of steel, steely rigid and unbendingly unimaginative, like the logic and theory of the Patriot who coldly and uncreatively compromises his person for an idea of a native land. The "self" that the patriot–theorizer creates or accepts is worked out by the calculations of the intellect, unlike the "spell" worked out and experienced by the lover–poet that is the creation of "Affection" and "Genius" (seen in conjunction with the Latin sense of "attendant spirit" or the "something about a thing that makes it particularly itself"; see also L651). I think it is important to be clear that for Dickinson, in mature work, this network of metaphor of "magic" did not represent in any way the poet's personal daemonic power (though she was well aware of the existence of such a thing, and that it was a kind of madness) but, on the contrary, her genuine and increasing sense of the essential subjecting mysteriousness of the 'poetic' itself, as it permeates perceiver and perceived in relationship. See also, I think significantly in conjunction with this passage, Coleridge (contemplating his relationship to Asra), *Notebooks*, III, 3708: "I inevitably by some link return to you . . . or bring some fuel of thought to the ceaseless Yearning for you at my inmost . . . I began strictly and as a matter of fact to examine that *subtle Vulcanian Spider-web net of Steel—strong as Steel yet subtle as the Ether, in which my soul flutters inclosed with the Idea of your's*—to pass rapidly as in a catalogue thro' the Images only, exclusive of the thousand Thoughts that possess the same force, which never fail instantly to awake into vivider flame the for ever and ever Feeling of you—" (my emphasis).

adding another dimension of complexity to the understanding, and the maturer the work, I suggest, the greater this possibility is.[117] One recalls her parable in L353 to Higginson (c. late October 1870): "Experiment escorts us last—. . . A Beggar came last week—I gave him Food and Fire as he went, 'Where do you go,' 'In all the directions'", replies her beggar/barefoot one/poet, evoking her "centre-to-circumference" idea of the poet's effort.

---

[117] See Coleridge, *Notebooks*, III, 3789: "Words in original Languages are really sentences, each syllable certainly being a distinct symbol; but very often each letter being the relict of a syllable—perhaps of several", regarding this quality of Dickinson's words gradually attaining to the richness and complexity of art-symbols in themselves. This may have something to do with capturing deeper, more primitive levels of experience, both to make these levels available for use, but also, in their "fixing" (L251), to give them that "calming power [on the Passions] which all *distinct* images exert on the human soul" (4397; draft of his brilliant 13th Philosophical Lecture, 10 March 1818); and again: "Art itself might be defined, as of a middle nature between a Thought and a Thing, or . . . the union and reconciliation of that which is Nature with that which is exclusively Human. . . . ". See also, in above context, I. A. Richards (*Practical Criticism*, note 198, 218): "No one who uses a dictionary—for other than orthographic purposes—can have escaped the shock of discovering how very far ahead of us our words often are. How subtly they already record distinctions towards which we are still groping. And many young philologists and grammarians must have indulged dreams of bringing some of this wisdom into the ordered system of science. If we could read this reflection of our minds aright, we might learn nearly as much as about ourselves as we shall ever wish to know: we should certainly increase enormously our power of handling our knowledge. Many of the distinctions words convey have been arrived at and recorded by methods no single mind could apply, complex methods that are, as yet, not well understood . . .". And see Iain McGilchrist (*Against Criticism*, London: Faber and Faber, 1982) from another (more currently favoured) vertex: "It will be becoming increasingly apparent as we go on that the real importance of literature lies not in its explicit meanings, but in what is not, and cannot be, said—in a sort of speaking silence; . . . not just any silence—what stands round and defines that silence is all-important; but the meaning of the work exists none the less in the gaps, the interstices and vibrant spaces between the apparent components of the solid structure offered, not in the components themselves. §The meaning of the words which compose the work does depend on the primitive significations of the words taken out of context. But it does so rather as a window depends on a window-frame. The window itself is simply the space between. In art the meaning too exists in the space, the relations, between those words when they are put together to form a unique whole. It exists in the gap where no word speaks."

We go into the second line (l. 5), where the insistence of the rhythm and tightness of sounds sustains the sense of rigour, unlike in the third and fourth lines (ll. 7–8). The personification of Nature suggested in the metaphor of the worn Afternoon (relating to the judgement–Patriot image) is continued. Here Nature "squanders", as a spendthrift might, in lending out this "austere Afternoon" to a person who cannot appreciate it; "Rigor" picks up the shades of barren judgement suggested in the first sentence—the rigour of obtuse or oversimplified law, the rigour of lack of imagination and partiality, rigor mortis and the death of meaning in life. Again, the rigour of the truth (like "test's severe repairs", L330, that test our fictions, and the "Heavenly Hurt" of before) may be in the wings, and the sense of it being "squandered" be thus that she is incapable of rising to face the truth of this experience—all is still struggling and in the balance. Of course there is also bitter irony in it, connected to the first of these options: rigour being squandered is oxymoronic, as 'generous cruelty' might be (again her words breaking their logical boundaries). The punctuation of the moment in "—now—" gives "love" a half-rhyme, as it were recalling these concepts to one another, setting up the irony of the contrast between the "squandered Rigor" of the bitter present and the formerly "squandered Love". On the one hand, the "squandered Love" of the past makes the surplus of "rigor" now seem doubly cruel. On the other hand, it makes the love of before, as if it "spoiled her for a ruder love" (L246), logically senseless—squandered indeed—and does not simply express the *largesse* of the father–friend's life. "What made fatuous sunbeams toil to break earth's sleep at all?" in Owen's words, to be "murdered" in another one of that Corporation God's many paralysing wars.[118]

Both these shades of meaning within the line, however, lead on the idea of the austerity of before, perhaps robbing it of its ambiguity as an instructive or meaningful austerity to some extent, and adding to it a shade of vileness and fatuity indeed in the engulfing depression that seems to take over the writer. To emerge in the looser third line: "Chastening—it may be—/ the Lass that she

[118] L256: "Austin is chilled—by Frazer's murder". His father paid for him to get out of it (Sewall, *Life*, 536).

receiveth", where the hard sounds and insistent rhythm of the lines dissolve and come apart like melting snow being crunched beneath a foot, and where the due solemnity of the Biblical words becomes an odd mixture of softness and crispness. The effect is helped by the preponderance of 'a'-based vowel sounds and the absence of such hard consonants as there were in the previous line (b, v, d, n), while the 's' sounds become less spiteful and snakelike under the influence of the archaic "-eth" and suggest, if not simply softness, then a more brilliant, pure clarity (like the 'candid' sense in 'chaste').

It is also worth having a look at what she has done to the source.[119]

> My son, despise thou not the chastening of the Lord.
> Nor faint when thou art rebuked of him:
> For whom the Lorde loveth, him he chasteneth,
> And scourgeth every son whom he receiveth.

She has contracted the Biblical source, taking much of the direct brutality out of the quotation (removing "scourgeth", and changing the Lord to a feminine Nature, as it were Mother Earth). The association of Nature with the Lord, however, recalls the same tendency as resides in the proximity of the austere Afternoon to the Judge and moment of judgement. Perhaps like the Bible, and certainly with typical poetic economy, her "receiveth" seems to suggest "loveth" to some extent, also the sense "to receive a guest or a person to be judged" (the image of the guest being an important one in her metaphor),[120] as well as the sense of "who dies, goes back to nature" albeit in a mitigating aspect, rather as the Father is to be seen tenderly tucked up and encapsuled in the "marl House". And this last again would bring out the intransigence of the austerity, steeliness, spellbound frozen quality of the experience she is undergoing, as if it were silently creating her death, sending her back to Nature, like Dust to Dust.

---

[119] *Hebrews*, 12:6. Structurally it seems to be an ancestor of P1393 relating to her father.

[120] See, for example, P1540; her word-portrait L268. See also Section I.2 and note 92 above.

But this third line, in dissolving, also seems to bring out the equivocal quality of the austerity and spell, if rather doubtfully and wearily. "Chastening" contains 'scolding' and more fundamentally 'rendering pure, purging', as in the Bible. These link back to the "austere", the "Steel", the "Rigor". But its sound and possibly the idea of purity and candid whiteness look forward to the image of the Snow, and the suggestion of melting that can be developed from this metaphor (as well as others—star, light, and so on—which bring out a different potential in the snow, and which I discuss below); and to the images of the gentle, pregnantly deep sleeping that pervades as the letter is overwhelmed by depressive feelings and milked of its brutally self-damaging bitterness; and as it turns to enquiring, and to the search for knowledge of the world, where love of it is not possible.

Thus with the emphatically placed "Chastening"—a participle after a full-stop with its subject held hostage in the preceding sentence—the first meaning we pick up is 'scolding', the shadow of the Bible's "scourging". But then the minute and precariously inserted "it may be" (rather similar in function to the 1861 letter's "perhaps that's what alarms") both gives us the sense 'purifying' and doubts it simultaneously. Or, rather: it casts the doubt—and since we do not doubt the "scourging" sense of "Chastening" in the context, we are forced to elicit the 'purifying' root of the word, and to doubt that. But in a sense the doubt is too late: the balance has turned. With the homely and gentle naming of the "Lass" we are already in a different and elegiac register, perhaps recalling Guiderius' song in *Cymbeline* (IV. ii. 262–263). Elsewhere Dickinson wrote that "'Whom he loveth, he punisheth' is a doubtful solace finding tart response in the lower Mind" (L369). Here one might say she is working out what "solace" can really mean, what of it is really possible, and what that possibility involves. Again she is working away from the Company–Patriot and from the fixed idea of the orthodox comfort of the "solace" of the afterlife and of "Redemption", as in the letters of the 1860s, "seeking what [the words] mean" (L815), and what the "things" are.

So, with the entry of sadness into the ideas and structure of the line, the "steeliness" begins to give. The last line of the verse (l. 8) seems to bring the cry to a whisper: "My House is a House of Snow—true—sadly—of few". Again the sound of the line is soft because of the many vowels, the 's's under the force of the 'h's again calm to a gentle half-rhyme that echoes internally (true–few), possibly, as I have suggested, picking up the word "Love" before; and the many divisions created by the dashes almost suggest a breakdown or dissolution of connections, leading into the sleeping images that follow. This seems to me the more the case in that "true—sadly—of few" seems to be illogical as well as structurally dissolved, and I will look at this after the "House of Snow".

The "House" obviously refers to her family, and as such has a ring to it as if it were, for example, the "House of Atreus", reflecting back on the "Land" of before as if it had meant "realm". And as before "my sole Land" was "my Friend", it is as if here the "House of Snow" were something to do with this friend's being dead/deeply asleep in sorrow or thought. The "House" also seems to suggest 'my self' (therefore 'in my particular body', like the Anglo-Saxon 'bone-house': body/cage of earthly form), in that it seems to refer very particularly to *her* "House" (not "the House" as later, for example), in a similar way to the pictures of her family in the 1861 letter being *her* pictures. And thus, since it is of "Snow", it seems to be descriptive of her own mental dissolution or going into a deep sleep that she seems to be observing in herself in the letter, perhaps as she guards her internal people, in the anger with and transformation of, or distinguishing different parts of, the austerity. Even in the 1861 letter, one saw the suggestion of the "House" as the image of the body or receptacle in which some guest, quality, or experience could be received (the Butterfly-in-the-Morning-Glory there; the dead-in-the-Snow-marl-House here), where it could be met, or known, as Nature austerely receives the Lass to her Doom–Judgement here in the process of assimilating the experience of the loss of her father and in a sense the disruption and statelessness of her whole family. All "Emigrants" again, as it were, in this context linking to the image of the migrant "birds" in a poem in L278.

One might also look for a moment at a poem, perhaps written three years later, though very possibly about the same time:

Go not too near a House of Rose
The depradation of a Breeze
Or inundation of a Dew
Alarm it's walls away
Nor try to tie the Butterfly,
Nor climb the Bars of Ecstasy,
In Insecurity to lie
Is Joy's insuring quality.[121]

Here the "House *of Rose*" seems to represent the fragile, delicate treasure, the ecstasy that can be alarmed to pieces, blown apart (like a literal rose) at any moment by a Breeze (linked to the "Wind" discussed before?) seen in a menacing aspect, like the faith attacked by the Dust of the 1861 letter. In our letter, it is as if the "House of Snow" were even too far without the possibility of such an attack: there is "No Event of Wind or Bird"—on the contrary, the wish is that there might be. There is no danger of an "ecstasy" or ecstatic faith collapsing, but the need for an austerity or close-fisted scepticism to be suppled, the spell of Steel to be "broken" (a word that theoretically keeps within the common metaphor—to break a spell—but stretches it by evoking its concrete origins to demonstrate the brutality of the state). The snow, then, seems to link partly to the austerity of before—the steel, rigor (frozen, freezing cold, sharply brilliant), to the "Chastening" (sharply brilliant, pure white). But it also adds the possibility (connected to its safety from being collapsed like the ecstasy) of melting, of tears, the suggestion of a deep, necessary, dreamlike sleep, as if in winter hibernation beneath the snow and robes of Mother Earth; and so it carries us into the next images.[122]

---

[121] L558. The "Bars" and reference in the letter may also be linked to Jacob's ladder (*Genesis* 28:12) that emerges in Milton's imagery (*P.L.*, III, 516–517), possibly related to Homer's golden chain, as chain/ladder linking universe to Jupiter/earth to Heaven, creative of order in things.

[122] It is worth looking at other contexts of her use of the image of SNOW, and related images, both before and after the 1875 letter, which bear on the images in the text. It seemed capable of representing death, marriage, rebirth, purity, for example:

As I said before, "—true—sadly—of few" seems broken up in such a way that all logical sense pours out of it, and all we are left with are the disconnected bits that belong, not to each other in any way (unlike the heavily hyphenated words and syntagms of some of her work in the 1860s), but to other sense units that are lost. It is as if the very structure of the words is going into a deep sleep. One can try to see what the sense of the sentence is, even what its ambiguities might be, since her statements are rarely simple at this stage. But nothing gives. Suppose one saw the "House of Snow" in its crueller aspect, relating to finite death and the crushing severity

---

We are the birds that stay,
The shiverers round farmers' doors,
For whose reluctant crumb
We stipulate, till pitying snows
Persuade our feathers home. [L278]

Here the "pitying snows" seem to represent the kindness of death in an intolerable situation—they take us to death, yes, but they take us "home". Or take: "I fear we all have sorrow, though of different forms—but with Life so very sweet at the Crisp, what must it be unfrozen!" (L472), where the snow latent in the "Crisp" (poetically more capable than "frozen") seems a representation of pain-in-life, austerity, transformed into something positive, vital; while "unfrozen" seems to suggest death but also immortality, as if you come alive ('defrost', become supple) when you give up life (crisp and punchy, but rigid). Or take the image of the flake falling to the ground as of the dead person falling to his death, ceding to Life's "declivity" (P420), in the beautiful metaphor of her mother's dying:"she slipped from our fingers like a flake gathered by the wind and is now part of a drift called 'the infinite' (L785). This image links to images of the bird falling (e.g. L724, L779), with source in *Hamlet* (V. ii. 229–233), and of the star's "Ascension" (P967, P970) which I discuss later in the text. In its connection with "white", snow seems also to represent death, marriage, and rebirth (see for example coming "in white", L233); and thus, in turn, to connect to the images of "Light" (the "Prism" divides the white ray of Light into all colours, thus possibly connecting to her use of Blue, Pink, Purple as metaphor), and to the images of "Star", which I discuss in the text and in whose context it seems to arise again particularly around 1875 with our letter and thence to continue. It therefore also links to the idea/image of Light's "Departure" connected to death and to rebirth in the same way as Summer departed "into the Beautiful", and it is "by their departure" that the "great confidences of Life" are disclosed to us, in turn linked to the question of those who "have Power to us" leaving "no mode", but inspiring us to find a mode each of our own to reach them or establish them "within".

of the experience: "true—sadly—of few" might approximate to "Unfortunately more people are not in this dreadful condition", an unlikely comment. Its melting aspect, the sense of its recognition of grief and possibility of crying, meaning 'a pity more people aren't capable of crying' seems more possible. But the progress of the words does not seem to me to have reached the stage in the letter yet—if it ever does—where such an externally observing comment on the outside world could be made. It obviously links to the later "I trust [the New Year] is whole and hale—to you", and the sense of desolation engulfing her (as if, as is statistically unlikely if irrelevant to her personal world, no one else had ever died and no other daughter ever suffered such a loss). And it seems to me that, in a dislocated way, the sentence started out intending to state that this was: "true of few" (to the many others the year is whole and hale), but "sadly" interposed in the light of "true" alone and the recognition that she was sad about her house being "of Snow", before it could make a bridge to "of few". It is also possible that the sense is "my house is of snow, true sadly, it's a house now of few persons since the brother and father are not in it". But in any case, I think, none of these possible interpretations distracts from the apparently accidentally dislocated quality of the sentence as a whole, the effect of dislocation that the structure conveys.

At last we move into her sleeping House (l. 9). One of the striking things about it is how the father is included with the living, and the living seem close to the dead (as in the star–asterisk image that develops later), in spite of elements of separation that I discuss below. The writing falls back into quiet prose. The one predicate, "asleep",[123] links the three figures (she seems the thinking, observant, protective eye awake, the snow covering the "marl House"). Only with the picture of the father does a particular rhythm pick up again in the alliterated "—in the Masked Bed—in the marl

[123] Not the same part of speech, in fact, as 'dead', it has, however, a similar finite quality—as against 'sleeping' for example—and in Middle English was used for meaning 'dead'. See also *Acts*, 13:36 for use of adverbial phrase 'on sleep', from which it seems to derive (*OED*).

House", which takes off into the delicate, comet- or lost-star-like quatrain imaging his sleep in very particular detail.

In another sense, though, and simultaneously, these images joining the dead to the living or suspending them all in a single capsule for a time also seem to contain images of their separation. This is really present in the "Masked Bed" and "marl House" already: these mitigate the hard truth in that they give a tolerable "face" in metaphor—like the death-mask or "Mold" would give the illusion of our still possessing our loved—to an intolerable pain, enabling her to set up a workable contact with an idea that is otherwise too much to bear. And, as I have indicated above, possibly the imaging of the snow covering the marl ground suggests her thinking about/cradling/cherishing his lost face.[124] But on the other hand the face "masked" clearly shows precisely the absence of the specific "face", the specific earthly form "that sees—and steps—and touches" (L678), yet to be recuperated in some other unknown and possibly definitively unknowable form. Equally the "marl House" of the metaphor (linked to the clay-dust image from the Bible later, though she may have got the word as such from Milton, *P. L.*, I, 296) separates him from the house "of Snow" that can melt eventually and makes him, in a sense, the "lost" (e.g. L873) object of the search I mention throughout.

But what emerges time and again, even starting with the discussion of the House of Snow earlier, is the suggestion of the image of the star, traditionally a poetic image of the living soul and influencer of living men's lives.[125] In the quatrain, this association seems to me created partly by the sense of the exaltation of the image the lines give, which is similar to that in L967 and L1043: (looking at her father's portrait at the top of the stairs)

> Go thy great way!
> The Stars thou meetst
> Are even as Thyself—
> For what are Stars but Asterisks
> To point a human Life?

---

[124] Cf. the image of the "angel with its needle toil [ing] beneath the snow", in L435.

[125] See also, for example, her use of the *idea* of the lode-star in L645.

and (of Helen Hunt Jackson's death):

The immortality she gave
Was borrowed at her Grave—
For just one Plaudit famishing,
The Might of Human Love—

The sweet Acclamation of Death divulges it—
There is no Trumpet like the Tomb—

Of Glory not a Beam is left
But her Eternal House—
The Asterisk is for the Dead,
The Living, for the Stars—

The subtle intermingling of the stars and asterisks, the living and the dead here is certainly worth keeping in mind, also, I suggest, in relation to the interchangeability we saw earlier in the identity of the sender/recipient, the male/female and the becoming of "it".[126] Partly, however, it develops retrospectively from the "firm Light" that will follow, and the link this has to what seems to me a network of metaphor that develops interlacing the image of the star, Light (though this like Milton's God an 'image' difficult or impossible to visualize, "leaving no mode") white/snow/snowflake–star.

These images develop and gradually meet and cross and leave each other like Keats' "tapestry Empyrean" in the network of her metaphor.[127] But all have to do with this apparently central theme developing of the possibility of discovering beauty being to do with apprehending your powerlessness over what you love and find beautiful, except in so far as you may improve your own relationship to it, protect it from your "ravenousness" (L824), or worse. This involves loving its freedom, loving your own pain at its being free (also to die, like her father here), since this is a sign of its being so. This also seems to involve the sparking-off of the search to establish an "internal" (L525) relationship (like the "June when the Corn is cut whose Option is within") to that object or

---

[126] See P1605, also in L891: "Each that we lose takes part of us; / A crescent still abides, / Which like the moon, some turbid night, / Is summoned by the tides", working a related metaphor.

[127] Letter to Reynolds, 19 February 1818.

"Dream" it becomes, in the sense that this is the beginning of the object's/beauty's immortality, and this search thus represents both a tribute to the object (in the most fundamental sense, a "thank you in [the] Heart", L955), as well as the beginning of the shaping of the identity—the real as opposed to the purely imitative and parasitic existence—of the live person's/rememberer's own life. The poet, in particular, gradually finds the "chiefest words" and 'chiefest objects' that are sought outside but no longer seen in quite the same way or context. As she does so, she uses these to explore, articulate, and distinguish between different states and relationships (Emigrant–Jesus, Emigrant–Judas, "meddler" L893, or saviour), primarily within herself, but this as a pattern of all men. In this process she conducts an enquiry into the relationship between word and object and as to how to keep both alive—that is, meaningful—in their relationship to each other. For example, the "emigrant" is herself: the "Emigrant" cast out from her Home is the "poet" seeking the truth internally. But the "Emigrant" is also the "false fleer" who 'mis-takes' her Home in her method of trying to reach it. Perhaps this "poet" is also that (linked by the common metaphor or images allied to it), perhaps the false fleer or Judas within is always a lurking possibility and an inevitable part of that "knowing ourselves" through which we may learn to distinguish the true flight "Home", the true meeting, "it". This pervading idea of the significance of the quality of the interrelationship between self and object was what made Dickinson the inheritor of the Romantics, I believe.

In this letter, then, while it is clear that she is shaken by her father's death, it is also clear that she is not totally unprepared: that she has experimented with this knowledge before and does not regard his death—the final physical losing him—any more as part of some other life, totally strange and fundamentally different from this one she is living now. She has lived loving him knowing she would lose him ("we missed him while he was with us and missed him when he was gone"); and knowing that loving meant knowing he would be lost, and that her "Business" was not to get lost first (in the end she would "sit down" with dignity, P247) but to "love" and to "sing" (L269), even in the midst of "dissolution" (L685), to establish that figure, like "*my* George Eliot", within. So that when he commits that "Act" that is "distinctly of the Spirit" (and not just indistinctly so, a temporary physical absence, "playing at Paste", P320), he begins to live in her in a sense, like the "Word" that "is dead / When it is said / Some say. I say it just / Begins to live / That day" (P1212).

Apparently a talented pianist, she liked musical metaphors. We saw elsewhere how she experienced her friends in this metaphor of their meeting: "those melodious moments of which friends are composed" (L969). Here is how she addressed the absent Helen Hunt Jackson:

> Pursuing you in your transitions,
> In other Motes—
> Of other Myths
> Your requisition be.
> The Prism never held the Hues,
> It only heard them play—

It is as if the absent friend and her relationship to her has become simply music in another key or a bridge section of the same piece ("transition"). The tone is so akin to these quatrains and images searching for the lost beloved, for their form, their abode, that Helen Hunt Jackson might as well have been dead, or the dead (like her father) alive. And the image of the prism holding the hues (also linking to the image of light and the star, as well as to the suggested instrument "housing" the musical notes and pauses;[128] to the butterfly-and-flower house of before; or to the image–act biography recounts of Dickinson standing behind the door ajar listening to Mabel Loomis Todd's singing) seems to express this relationship of the loved object found within. It simultaneously seems to express the mode,[129] which the "Light" that has "Power to

---

[128] See also L418, where she calls her father after his death a "pause of space".

[129] "Mode" seems suggested here as part of the musical metaphor. The "mote" she has in fact used must be the dust particle, though it may also link to the bugle note, and seems to suggest—in its link here to the star image (other motes/myths/Hues-all colours therefore white Light)—the living souls of the dead, the immortal parts that are about us in the air, towards which we tend and are pulled by the "Might of Human Love". It is of course linked to the image suggested in Section II.2 above, where the Dust seemed to be seen in/around a light, but it is seen in a persecutory aspect there.

us" does not and cannot provide for us, being found in the act of establishing this relationship, this container for the lost or to-be-lost object. This, in turn, evokes both the awful beauty of the object ("it only heard [the Hues] play") and our subjection before it and "near-ness" to it in finding it, as well as its "far-ness": that is, the impossibility of becoming or possessing it ("the Prism never held the Hues").

So, to return to the images of the snow/white/star/light: as we saw in the poems quoted above relating to the "Star", this image seems to stand for the "Ascension" and brilliance of the lost beloved. In those particular images (later than those we are dealing with in the letter), the image is played against that of the "Asterisk". Simply on one level, an asterisk looks like a dead, two-dimensional star; on paper it also signals something left out but possibly essential to the main text (again the image of the internal figure, though perhaps a dead internal figure?), the sign of the life-that-was, as the star light is also the sign of an explosion that was,[130] but in "Fact" is now a "Fiction",[131] an optical illusion, as it were, but potentially of great significance and use to us. The revolution that she works on the metaphor for Helen Hunt Jackson, as I said above, brings the dead to the living and vice versa even more intensely, rather similarly but more vitally than the moon-crescent image mentioned earlier (see note 126 above). Whereas before the freed Star ("Go thy great way!") was the dead man, and she could link him to earth and the living by the asterisk pointing to the "pause of Space" where he used to be, here she seems to leave the asterisk behind altogether. The "Dead" seems to mean anyone not with Helen and her "Eternal House" that we "borrow at her Grave". It seems to refer more to the spiritual division between death and life than to the physical division, as if it said "those who die spiritually can keep the asterisk", the sign of the "missing person". Meanwhile the beautiful shift of the structure in the last line (putting the Dead next to the Living and upsetting the expected symmetry of the antithesis) seems to make Helen into a star

[130] Cf. Shelley (*A Defence of Poetry*): "the mind in creation is as a fading coal, which some invisible influence, like an inconstant wind, awakens to transitory brightness".

[131] L653: "which was the Child of Fiction, the Child of Fiction or of Fact, and is 'Come unto me' for Father or Child, when the Child precedes?"

who is less representable by an asterisk now than the human living may be who, on the contrary, tend towards her (the Living journey towards the Stars, towards that object and the immortality she gives "at her Grave"—as she escapes forever, by her departure—instead of leaving a 2-dimensional asterisk). Becoming alive means going towards death ("for the Stars"), but it simultaneously seems to mean not looking for a sign marking deadly the place you were (Stars stand for the Living), but striving towards a state of true immortality that can be passed on in progressive transformation, not just mirrored flatly. As in the moon-crescent image, there is the suggestion of the tidal pull between the living and the dead, the "Might of Human Love" that forever pulls between spirits that have loved; but more, here, there seems to be this image conjoined to it of immortality.

To return, then, to the quatrain in the letter (l. 11) more specifically. Full of painful contrasts that seem to pick up the contrasts and dissonances earlier in the letter, it seems to attempt even more intensely to assimilate and transform the intransigently bitter aspects of her experience of her father's death. The antithtetical positions in the form and the antithetical meanings of the words—soft/Prison, sweet/sullen Bars, Despot/King of Down—create a capsule of tension that seems to contain the incomprehensibility of the antitheses. How can a prison be soft? how can sullen Bars be sweet? or a Despot a King of Down? "Soft" seems to pick up the gentle quality of the alliteration in the "House of Snow" line, softening the vowel sounds as well ("how soft"). It possibly links to it also in the sense of the "Snow" being connected to things frozenly-still-in-death; and yet snow is soft to lie on or could present a soft covering if we see the image as we saw it earlier: the father in the marl House under the snow covering that was also the snow of her desperate and protective state that might, however, melt, become more "liquid". And this is another word that comes into her imagery in the arc of time of these other images, with interesting resonance. For example, "I wish I might say one liquid word to make your sorrow less", and "Your sweet self-reprehension makes us look within, which is so wild a place we are soon dismayed, but the seed sown in the lake bears the liquid flower, and so of all your words" (L859, L860), as if it were linking the idea of the tear to the seed of regeneration, the end to the beginning. "Soft" also has something, however, of the Shakespearean "soft!" ("quiet!"), looking forward to the "sullen" and of course to the King of Down and his "repose"; it also branches out into to her ideas elsewhere of "clandestineness" and "whispering" in the church of life's mystery, as in a sense she seems to be doing here, as she seeks to find, and also to create, the meaning of the event.

The image of the "Prison", although brutal, is also mitigating, firstly, in the sense that it continues the idea of his life, his intermingling with the living, linked to the question of the star–asterisk intermingling and being distinguished before, and the equivocal quality of the words 'life'/'death' in relation to the Fact of being alive/being dead, and then also in its link to her experimentation with the idea of "Captivity", "Chillon" (L1042, L233, L249, L293) and different forms of being contained elsewhere in her work, where prison may be irritating and agonizing but it is decidedly not Death. This equivocal quality continues in the sweet–sullen Bars that follow (l. 12), still linked to the steel, rigorousness, and so on, of before. One can see this in the possibly later poem quoted above, in the "Bars of Ecstasy", for example, that she advises us not to climb, against her own practice. The "Bars" seem capable of a quality of prison-bars (that cruelly and kindly shut us in), and a quality of ladder-bars (that kindly and cruelly let us climb to the skies, like the soaring bird or star). I wonder if there is not also the suggestion of a rib-cage latent in the image as well, which again would recall the "chest to put the Alive in" and suggests the closeness of this to the Heart, where ecstasy—at peril—may be wrought in the relationship between the person with the capable chest/heart and the person who comes "in white"; between the flower that can contain the butterfly, between the poet and the divinity that "instructs the hand lightly created". The idea of the rib-cage seems relevant to me also because it seems again to contain the image of physical death as well (skeleton–death skull) that seems at play in the ambiguity and equivocalness of the images in her uncertainty as to whether this experience is killing or "expanding" her,[132]

[132] Cf. to Prose Fragment 49: "'Tis a dangerous moment when the meaning goes out of things and Life stands straight—and punctual—and yet no content (s) (signal) come (s). Yet such moments are. If we survive them they expand us, if we do not, but that is Death, whose if is everlasting." It seems to me you can

equally as to whether the dead can live on, and if so, in what form, in what relation to her, for as long as it remains her lot be one of the living that must learn to be "Alive"? Only one letter remains to indicate that she prosaically and directly asked about the doctrine of "Immortality".[133] But if one were to make an abstraction of a burning question in her writings, it would be that.

Here, then, the shadow of death is present, but is harnessed, even sweetly, by these words, and the seed of the search for the lost can set in: the rigour of the opening is shifted slightly, and the image of death can enter without overwhelming totally, so that by the time we get to the "No Despot" (l. 13) that structurally echoes the earlier "No Event of Wind or Bird", the significance seems to have been reversed—the "spell of Steel" has become "that Repose". The softness of the Prison is picked up again in the "Down", while perhaps just as the poem "My Life had stood—a Loaded Gun" (P754) shows us that "softness" can be as treacherous as a letter-gun, or the storm of any meeting, it retains, defused, the image of Death in a pun (like the falling "Down" of the bird or the "eloquent lying" in death of the snowflake that the wind has "exasperated", L472, L724, L779). And "Repose" relates to the image of the sleeping that unites them all, and to the masking of the brutality of death in the image of the father lying at rest on something soft; while it also admits of death as the Finalizer of Occasions, just as P465 could suggest that it was as "harmless as a fly–Bee", given the ambiguity of that creature.

Thus there seems to be a deep control over the image of the death and her emotions concerning it, but it seems to have become more articulate and less frozen in the course of the letter. The precise tone of the quatrain, indeed, seems to me rather difficult to

---

see the shadow of the Company man working the almost allegorical image of Life (straight and punctual) here, this being another device she grew to have real genius with (cf. figure of "Love" in L536). Life that is "straight", all present and correct and according to the Company rules, is Life without meaning, is Death. In all this area of imagery, Golgotha (skull), Gethsemane and the Calvary Cross, with the three steps (stairs/bars) leading up to it, are never far away. The "Company" issue is ghosted by the dynamics of the betrayal and crucifixion scenes in the Bible (*John*).

133 L752a, from Washington Gladden. But many of her letters are lost to us, and perhaps, as Luce portrays (Preface to *The Belle of Amherst*), the "great words" of the Christian religion formed at least part of the lost letters to Wadsworth.

gauge and fairly complex. There may be a level of deep irony in it, or at least the possibility of this. It is interesting to see the (subsequent?) changes to the first quatrain and then the entire second one in P1334, a sort of variation on the Biblical "Death where is thy sting?" which she quotes in L967: "where is thy Chancellor", perhaps yet another variation on the Company figure, the divider of lovers, as he stands at the gates:

> How soft this Prison is
> How sweet those sullen bars
> No Despot but the King of Down
> Invented this repose
>
> Of Fate if this is All
> Has he no added Realm
> A Dungeon but a Kinsman is
> Incarceration—Home.

This does not make the problem any easier; if anything, it complicates the meaning. She seems to be talking, not only about physical death (as she was in the letter quatrain), but, in the same breath, about physical life. This Prison—her life; these sullen Bars—her body/bone-house that cages the spirit, again recalling the skeleton-skull image. "This repose" could be an (ironical?) euphemism for the brutal finality of Death the Divider. But it also seems linked to the "interval" between experience and the "most profound experiment / Appointed unto Men" (P822), which is a poetical development of the Biblical "we shall not all sleep . . . for the trumpet shall sound, and the dead shall be raised incorruptible" and in its heterodoxy, it seems to me, also to Wordsworth's idea of this life as "a sleep and a forgetting".[134] So the image could be of the body-imprisoned-in-life superimposed on the image of the body-imprisoned-in-death, both relating to the discovery of eternal life in some

[134] *Immortality Ode*, l. 58, more recently and perhaps more authentically entitled "Ode ('There was a time . . . ')" by editors such as Stephen Gill and Duncan Wu, who, in the last fifteen years, have concerned themselves much with bringing to public attention the significance to our understanding, of attention to the chronological development of the work of this poet. This line of the "Ode" probably owes much to the Duke's speech in *Measure for Measure*, III. i. 5–41.

way. And the first of these is certainly related to the idea of the coming alive that imagining dying can instigate, as in Plato's advice: "Practise dying".[135]

The second verse thus could suggest that Death/Fate has no sting, no Chancellor: between this life in the body where we practise dying and so learn to be alive, and that life without our body that is the continuum of all that is immortal, there is no real division. Death is really life without meaning, "where the meanings are" not, as it were—here or on the other side of that imagined portal. As such, on the one hand, the apparently interrogative structure: "Has he no added Realm", coming after the conditional clause: "if this is All", which arouses expectation of a statement of consequence, would seem rhetorical and exclamatory. An act of defiance and a victory over the "finish". And the last two lines, in the Incarceration/Prison, would continue the possibility of physical life in Verse One and suggest the body/bone-house and the breathing chest of before, the "Dungeon" is the "Kinsman", as the "Friend" is the "sole Land" in our letter. And again here there is the microcosm suggestion, in the light of comments such as "I begin to roam my Room now" (L1042), that her "Friend" is also her 'self'. So that earth/Incarceration (perhaps in the sense of the chest–Alive relationship) is our true "Home", rather than the illusory paradise/freedom of a hegemonic and fundamentally despairing idea, or the Home in the orthodox Afterlife, without the prison Bars of the body, but also without "sensible warm motion" and without the particular form, or the "cup" from which we drink "ecstasy", before we even begin to know what "it" is (L891; and see *John* 18:11).

On the other hand, the second verse seems capable of picking up the image of death as a final separation and physical life as a circumscribed moment that will end in every sense: "Of Fate if this is All there is [life ending in death] / Has he no added Realm [afterlife]"; and the interrogative structure of "Has he . . .", then, to be partly a flash of contemptuous rage and disillusion, such as in "Some new equation given—but what of that?" (P301). This perhaps moves to resignation and relief that the torments of life are over and the end has come of the prospect of the terribleness of the

---

[135] *Phaedo*, quoted in R. Weisbuch, *Emily Dickinson's Poetry*, Chicago and London: University of Chicago Press, 1975, 132.

despotic judgement of a tyrant—like the ambiguous "King" figure in P465—that we scare ourselves rigid with in life. Thus the "Dungeon" is the tomb; and "but a Kinsman is" takes on more the nature of simile than deep metaphor. A dungeon–grave is "*like* something in which we can feel at home", rather than "*is* that little Region to wander in" that a Friend or self-Friend (see L418) also is, where immortality is created and perpetuated.

This comparison does nothing to simplify the meaning of our letter quatrain for us, but perhaps it makes the possibility of sarcastic irony in the vision less likely in that however one sees it, Dickinson is trying to make a friend of the Prison, whether it is gentle death like sleep that at least rests her from life and the nightmare of crude and dogmatic judgement, or life–death that is vital and creative of immortality. And it leaves the rather deeper irony that grieving might throw up, in the face of the paradox of the final aspect of things (physical death) and our dependent love and continuous desire for them to remain as they are.

As it stands, when the letter goes on to discuss the loss openly for the first time ("When I think of his firm Light—quenched so causelessly, it fritters the worth of much that shines", l. 15), it certainly picks up this ironic possibility. The "firm Light" intensifies the metaphorical quality of the weather/landscape that began with the "austere Afternoon", really even relinquishing the literal aspect of the image for good; and, as I suggested before, it seems to be connected to the idea of the bright whiteness of the snow that develops from the steely austerity of the letter's opening and to begin the suggestion of the star/asterisk that mingles the living with the dead and guides the living to seek and represent their "lost". "Firm" has the concrete quality of, for example, the expression *terra firma*, and she uses it elsewhere (L368) abstractly to indicate stability and durability. A contrast to the former dangerous rigidity, to the soft misery of the melting/sleeping people, and to the dead man's "Repose", it affords a dip back into the earlier earthly reality as it cries out against the change. "Quenched" throws the naked-fire aspect of the "Light" into relief, giving it a slightly perilous aspect, as of a great conflagration or a ball of fire, perhaps tendering another link to the images of the star or the sun, seen at a distance or close-to in their different qualities of flame and light. And it also relates, I think, to her metaphors of flood, the great waters, and so on, that I have mentioned before. "Causelessly" (l. 16) is one of those "–less" words she was fond of inventing. Here it seems to contain, on the one hand, "without a cause", relating to her use of the word "accident" in comments like: "I found you were gone, by accident, as I find Systems are . . . and obtain no cause", or "These beloved Accidents must become more frequent".[136] Thus it seems in this sense to relate to the question of active receptivity and non-interference in life's "secret" and to her rejection of the idea of simple cause-and-effect in our mechanistic view of relationship between events.

On the other hand, "causelessly" seems also to contain, by echo of the commoner "–less" compound, "pointlessly". Thus it picks up the "squandering" of before and looks forward to the "frittering" to come. So that overall it seems both to attempt to absorb her father's death into the system of life's "secret" (linked to the sleeping/dreaming Awe at life's mystery that precedes it), which is at once more truthful and more optimistic than a more mechanistic approach to it; and yet also to vent her inevitable feelings about the loss (also a part of "truth") in echoing "pointless", and thus, by suggestion of the contrast, to give an indication of how much more consoling is a system of belief, however cruel, that enables one to think one can know and rationalize cause and effect. If her father's death had a point, a cause, if it were the effect of a *cause* and not cause-less or point-less, if he'd only deserved to have been struck down—at least then there would be some relief, some order, some possibility of power: as we bolster our fears with ideas of heaven, hell, just reward and punishment that the Company man (the priest, the father, for example) can mete out to us, as if he were God, or at least *somebody* were God. "Tell me its Name!" (L873). I would think it also contains her trenchant comment on the staggering illogicality of the argumentation in the trial of Christ scenes in the Bible (*John* 18:28–40; 19:1–22—who can follow the reasoning there?). In sum, it is the not knowing that is the source of life's beauty and our hope; it is the not knowing that may be the source of our despair. And then withal, even the beauty of it being "causeless" may be "pointless"—it is truly the "yeares midnight".

As I said, "fritters" picks up the "squandering" of earlier, and structurally seems to dissipate into pieces the "firmness" or

[136] L280 and L354.

haleness of the "Light", which is picked up again in "shines", yet again linking it to the star and sun images mentioned before. So the letter, as in a dream or "fiction", amidst the sleeping figures and the mitigating image of her dead father, has moved into the first direct mention of his death or going out, and direct questioning of the *meaning* of the event. And she seems simultaneously to insert it into a system of sense, or at least a system where sense can be sought, in the ambiguity of the words and structures of words that she uses.

This continues in the elliptical leap to the Biblical quotation ("'Dust unto the Dust' indeed—but the final clause of that marvelous sentence—Who has rendered it . . .", l. 17)—a shorthand easily accessible enough still today. And in the terms of the letter it links back to the "Land/Friend" and the Father in the fertile marl House prison (of clay: like us-not like us). When she calls "Dust unto the Dust" the "first clause" of a sentence, she is not exercising her capacity for grammatical analysis but evidently refers to the "resurrection". And she deliberately does not cite the term, it seems to me, as it were a phenomenon still so 'unrecognizable' to her consciousness that she cannot yet even take the initial step of putting a name to it, to enable the progressive investigation of hypothesis (see Baruzzi, note 156 below). The in©42tuition of that possibly "marvelous sentence" is still waiting for its Maker, for indeed no "close logical congruity . . . will ever bear up against a glaring incongruity in the Imagination" (Coleridge, *Notebooks*, 3959). Hence the ambiguity of the question: ". . . Who has rendered it" (l. 18)—"it", the "resurrection"; "it", the final—indeed the main—clause of the sentence. As Marianne Moore said: "She was not usual, but her need was the universal human one, never disguised. She saw no comfort in refusing to question that about which she wished most to be sure". Still, no words she cannot hold. And then only the chiefest. Washington Gladden's bland assurances can only have saddened her, one imagines. [137]

[137] For a source of the sentence, see *Daniel* 12:2; *Ecclesiastes*, 12:7; *Genesis*, 3:19, most probably this last. See in the light of other references to *Genesis*: L554, L1037. The other clause, coming later in the letter with reference to "Mystery", is also in I *Corinthians*, 15:51. See also Marianne Moore, "Review of Emily Dickinson's Letters" (January 1933) No. 41, *Poetry*, Chicago, 219–226.

Unable to "render it" herself, she goes on to present a "Dream" of her living father while he "sleeps in the dust" (*Daniel*, 12:2), softly awaiting some kind of awakening, perhaps the farewell to, and then recuperation of the "face" in some vital form. The little interlude is made with the words of Christ ("I say unto you", l. 19: see, e.g., *Matthew*, 24:2), himself also the "Word". Again, like those "of Power to us", he "leaves no mode": that is, it is not the specific ratiocinative content of what he says that holds her to him (as we know she rather disagreed with him),[138] but "something else". The eruption of this prophetic-sounding statement seems to link it back to his "firmness"; so too the "*militant* Accent" that "startles" one. And it perhaps distinguishes itself from the "austerity" before (though it recalls it as well) in also linking to the absent Bird or Wind that might startle enough to "break the spell of Steel", like the "alarm" of the 1861 letter. And it may also be linked to the "pugilistic Audacity" of Jacob wrestling with the Angel that I discuss further below (L1042; *Genesis*, 32: 24–32). After the gentle picture of his "Repose", it seems rather to cry out the incredibleness of such an emphatic being's ending: he would speak like Christ prophetically, his accent was startling and militant enough to waken us from Death, and now (understood) he is nothing, or at least, gone as that "Face" that enabled that "rendezvous" where the "Heart could be wooed". The courtship is over, as it were: the "marriage of true minds" must begin (L856, quoting sonnet 116).

But with "Forgive me if I linger on the first Mystery of the House . . ." (l. 21), Dickinson seems to shift into a different sphere again, moving even more than before in the letter outside the direct

---

[138] Cf. also to her underscoring of a passage in her edition of *Jane Eyre* describing Mr Rochester (quoted in *Leyda*, II, 101): "The humanities and amenities of life had no attraction for him—he lived only to aspire—after what was good and great, certainly . . . a steadfast bulwark for great interests to rest upon; but, at the fireside, too often a cold, cumbrous column, gloomy and out of place", where the similarity with the picture of her father—as, for example, in an early version in L72—seems to suggest she felt about him as about a blind man in certain respects, though she evidently deeply loved him. One can but refer, yet again, to the great service done by Griffin Wolff's biography (*Emily Dickinson*), among other things, in more widely illuminating Dickinson's family context.

personal pain of the experience, to comment and observe rigorously her own participation in it. "Forgive me" obviously suggests her awareness of proportion (he is not the only man who ever died, and perhaps his death does not matter to everyone in the same way that it matters to her). The "linger" most beautifully expresses the way she seems to be looking at 'life' and 'death' from different points of view (as she said of her Milton-born "Chivalry", "a shining Word though I dont know its meaning", L856 again), and so again creates proportion. It also seems to look back to the idea of the "Friend/Land" as the little Region to wander in of the beginning: as a friend wandering almost contemplatively in her relationship with her friend, she lingers affectionately (like the "waiting" of the earlier letter?), trying to get to know every aspect of her father. Before in the "Eyes and Hair", the "loved Steps", the hands that "touch" (L262, L752, L678); now in his departure, and perhaps most of all so. "The Supper of the Heart is when the Guest has gone" (L318), or, as she was to say later more strictly in the context of these images of the star, and of her Origin: "There is no trumpet like the Tomb" (L1043). There is such a plethora of beautiful images and statements elaborated from imaginative conjecture regarding this enquiring in her work, it seems almost absurd even to quote one, but see, for example: "It is strange that the most intangible thing is the most adhesive" (L515).

With her description of his death as a "Mystery", she seems to link back to the suggestion of the amazement before, in the sleeping, after the bitterness of the opening; also to the sense of wonder in the questioning: "Who has rendered it"; and, in a sense, the term seems to draw together, and to represent, a new theme in the letter, as I suggested near the beginning of this section. And with this, "My House" of the earlier line is made universal, as if "the House" here included other members of the household, interpolating to the rest of the world; and this in tune with the thrust throughout the letter to become able to estimate the proportion of the event, to see it in relation to more than just herself and her own despair, or to see it as more than just the "finish". Undoubtedly the "Mystery" has a literal source in the Bible (I *Corinthians*, 15: 51), which also links to the suggestion of the trumpeting Tomb mentioned above:

> Behold, I shew you a mystery; we shall not all sleep, but we shall all be changed in a moment, in the twinkling of an eye, at the last trump: for the trumpet shall sound, and the dead shall be raised incorruptible, and this mortal shall put on immortality . . .

Poetically and ideally, it picks up the unfinished sentence "Dust unto Dust" in its search to discover what immortality may be, and, as I said above, her dream or "fiction" of the sleeping people that seems also a step in the search. As always, her use of the quotation or quoted word, in her own context against her own experience, is the demonstration of her "trying it" (L471), seeing what the doctrines can or cannot mean, working them out in an original (new-and-old) way in relation to the "Facts" of life.

The "specific Mystery" (l. 22) that follows on seems to be counterposed to the "Mystery of the House" in some way, as "my House" also was. It (like the "distinct Bird", L457) regards herself, and to her is her own experiment, she shall need "no intercessor" (L417); the "mystery of the House" regards her, as it regards everyone, and the entire structure or constellation of everyone's relationship to another, presumably. Thus the "House" would seem to represent her own royal dynasty–family, as it were, but to extrapolate, again, to the whole of society, to regard the family that is the macrocosm of the mind of the individual and the microcosm of mankind.

In a sense, as in the little moon-crescent poem, it is as if the father's going into another "world" had taken part of the body of society away with it. This seems the significance of "but within this world". That is, we each individually through the attempt at knowledge of our selves ("It's specific Mystery—each Heart had before ") know mystery; but, since we cannot become bereft of part of ourselves in the same way that we can become bereft of a loved person (an essential part of our group / the world), this experience of loss (a part lost "without this world") is a totally new, incomprehensible, and, what is more, irreversible, thing: it takes a part of all of us, changes all of us, individually, and as part of the whole, forever. This is a mystery you can experience *only in relation to other people/the outside world, not in relation to yourself.* The "*specific* Mystery" seems related also to the question of the "face" or "form" that "never will come back" and, I would think, is connected to the photograph issue that arose in the earlier letter, and to the question of true or forgotten-false portraits in that. Here we seem to be dealing with something slightly different in that, more than questioning the precise earthly form and mystery of its beauty, she seems to be assuming her father's continuing in some way, and his continuing Action in her life—"the first Act distinctly of the Spirit" (ll. 23–24, possibly connected to the Acts of the Apostles).[139] So she is questioning the spiritual form, and this seems to me linked to the central question of finding the lost and establishing some relationship to them "within"; to the image of the star/asterisk/light. And, I would think, it also links back to the Geranium/Sultana image (thus to the "Emigrant" metaphor) and the suggestion of the "Light shining inwards" of the earlier letter; and so to what seems to me the distinctness of the internal/spiritual meeting (suggested by this) from the earthly meeting, where "specific Mystery" meets "specific Mystery",[140] despite the vital reciprocal importance of these at another level.

---

[139] See *Acts* 4:31, where the Apostles speak the "word of God with boldness" (related to the father being the "Word" in "I say unto you"), and are "filled with the Holy Ghost".

[140] Cf. Sewall's speculation as to the nature of Dickinson's relationship to Wadsworth: "In subsequent letters to C. Clark, she spoke of Wadsworth's 'mysterious face' and his 'momentous nature'; to know him 'was Life—'. It would seem that mystery faced mystery in the meeting of these two people, and this may have been part of the fascination for her" (*Life*, 453–454). As suggested before (see note 13 above) speculation as to the identity of the "Master"'s identity has become superseded by a more rational point of view. Still, a curiosity: J. E. Walsh, in *The Hidden Life of Emily Dickinson* (New York: Simon & Schuster, 1971), builds up a detective-story-like argument to qualify the hypothesis that "the man" in Dickinson's life was, long before the (extant) open love letters, Otis Phillips Lord: Walsh's evidence for this, apart from her various use of the word "Lord", is that the pencil-stub letter-poem "If it had no pencil", in which she obliquely calls herself "Daisy" (as she does in no other place but in "Master" letters L233 and L248) was sent to Lord. But Leyda (*Leyda*, II, 80) has the same letter sent to Bowles (27 July 1863); Johnson, as far as I can see, does not have it as sent either to Bowles or to Lord in the 3-volume *Letters*, though it is inserted as P921, c.1864, in the 3-volume *Poems*.

It is interesting to see how structurally that "first Mystery of the House" seems to counterpoint "My House is a House of Snow", both in sound and vocabulary; and the whole section from here to ". . . distinctly of the Spirit" (ll. 24–25) suggests the irregular whistling whispering buffeting blowing of the wind, by the alliteration of "s" and "h" sounds, and the uneven punctuation of their intervals, perhaps as if the "Rigor" were being broken up, or at least disturbed.

"Distinctly" seems to contain "decidedly", as if meaning this was an Act of pure Spirit, with nothing earthly corruptible mingled in it; perhaps also "distinctive", describing her father with his startling militant Accent that would allow no slacking; and also "distinct", in the sense of "separate, alone"—related to the first meaning: it is his first Act in which he is totally other and without them, and incapable of their habitual "rendezvous" in his earthly form. It is interesting, too, to see how the description of his "firm Light", though it logically means him alive-in-his-body, is closer in the metaphor to the "first Act distinctly of the Spirit", as if perhaps the poet were already working towards an internal image of him, in a way that the quatrain does not, but rather retains the "corruptible".

At this point (l. 25) Austin haunts the picture in this matrix of distance and separation, as if her brother, separated from her by marriage only to be separated again from his marriage, reminded her of her father separated from his family. What seems to me extraordinary is the quality of reference of the lines: "It seemed peculiar—pathetic—and Antediluvian. We missed him while he was with us and missed him when he was gone" (ll. 27–28); as if they were describing, in relation to the Father and Austin (both perhaps figures of "austere"-ness that commanded her deep compassion), in relation to the past state and the present state, a moment in time when no relationship was right any more, there was no longer any right structure for the relationships that existed: the whole state is unsettled. She had not wanted Austin to leave their family, but he left and it hurt; ironically deserted, he came back, but by then even that hurt—nothing could be as it had been originally, and the distortion in the attempt to get it back or experience it set back was as bad as, if not worse than, the original and continual pain of the loss. "Peculiar—pathetic—Antediluvian" (ll. 26–27)—

like dinosaurs. What might be a good sense of "Antediluvian" (referring to their childhood, before the flood-disaster had ever been), seems eaten up by its conjunction with "peculiar—pathetic", as in her affirmation: "If things do not progress they go backward, that is the law of Flood" (L415), as if the Flood was then simply only to be lived through all over again; the new state of things had failed in some way. As in a vacuum left by the father's death, Austin—unanchored anyway—is sucked back into them, as if he replaced the father, and yet not replacing him; as if he were the brother of the old family, and yet the father maintaining that family's state is not there: all athwart. But as I said, it is as if the comment referred to her father too. In the context, the idea of "missing" seems to grow straight out of missing the father (something she had previously said only indirectly and in metaphor, for example in the "Friend being her sole Land"). And the "when he was gone" also links more sensibly to him. Conveyed in the repetition of "missed . . . missed" in the perfectly antithetical structure of the sentence, the pathetic paradox it expresses so forcefully seems to capture in a nutshell something of the paradoxical feeling about the father (as prototype for all intimate relationship to Beauty) in the rest of the letter. When he was alive, he was as distant and awe-inspiring and startling as Christ, and the Antediluvian heart of the child,[141] appreciating this, yearned for a closeness that could not be had. And this seems an intrinsic part of loving the friend who also, however, is its "sole Land"—there are no substitutes, "just itself".[142] When he was dead, the vision of him was as of a paradox: distant (as in the starlike quatrain), and the missing him merely doubled when the necessity of finding him became more intense when more impossible. The opposite situation did not bring the opposite feeling like an equation nicely balancing out. Whatever the father "is", in his Action mixed of body and spirit, and in his Action distinctly of the Spirit, he is equally an object of mystery and longing awe. So that in the progress of the letter, she seems to have reached a point where she accepts the fact of her father's dying and never coming back

[141] Cf. L503: "Day is tired, and lays her antediluvian cheek to the Hill like a child". Cf. also L843 to see the metaphor at work later.

[142] L262, and cf.: "it has only its heart", in the 1861 letter.

(which she could not face when she tried to hold on to his dead image in the quatrain), and she comments on the perversity of trying to make him come back externally, even though it might be the greatest desire of her heart. And she tries to make some reckoning of what it was really like when he was alive anyway, and in what form the relationship has significance to her and to the family-world. This seems to me to be the force of "All is so very curious": things change and we don't want them to, and feel the good things should not; yet if they revert or do not change, we feel they are not alive. And yet our relationship to things is so paradoxical anyway—we are near each other, yet far; far, yet near.

So, having moved through an initial expression of rigid misery, of personal loss and a moment of attempting to recuperate the face almost literally and perhaps hold back change, the letter in this last section (starting "When I think of his firm Light . . .", l. 15) seems dedicated to working out the sense of the death with all the intellectual, emotional, and even physical power she has, and its universal significance: if this is like this for me, who am an example of all patterns, what is the true form of this continuum, in what aspect does it have any sense?

The final "thank you"s (l. 30), liberated for a moment from the contemplation of the event, seem not insincere, but wooden (as she was to say after her mother's death: "I have answered a few inquiries of love, but written little intuitively", L785). The way she takes the words "New Year" and makes them almost concrete ("that New Year" instead of, say, "wishing me happy New Year") is typical of the way she infused meaning and dramatic capacity into words. From there, she can see the "fracture" in it (invisible in a wish), and so go on from one image to another, gradually building up a network of meaning and a particular language, a "mode" in all the senses in which I have discussed it before. The "fracture" seems linked to the metaphor, latent in the letter, of cold rigidity that is only susceptible to being broken or fractured (whereas warmer things seem just to melt or disintegrate like liquids, and perhaps are capable of finding new form). The hard alliteration of the line seems to bear this out, like that of "breaks the spell of Steel"; though "fracture" is also the word she used for damage to the basic spinal structure of something (perhaps here the prison

Bars/body), and in her much-advertised observation to Higginson: "Men do not call the surgeon, to commend—the Bone, but to set it, Sir, and fracture within, is more critical" (L268). In this letter, the "fracture" does not seem to be "within" in quite the same way or only personal to her, as she feared it might have been then (1862), close to the beginning of her making herself a poet; nor, as she feared in the meeting with Mary Bowles, specific Mystery facing specific Mystery, in the 1861 letter. Again here, as in the "specific Mystery" distinct from the "first Mystery of the House", it seems a more universal and endemic fracture—a fracture not in herself but in the natural state of things, of the house, their human house, God's seasonal house—and perhaps in that sense more totally disarming.

Still, in so far as any degree of adjustment to this fracture is possible, it seems it, too, may only be made from within. And the "I trust it is whole and hale—to you" (l. 31), for the time being picks up again the sense of desolation and temporary separateness from happier "houses" of the earlier "true—sadly—of few", as she concentrates on the possibility of "repair" perhaps, not just for herself but for her whole family-world as well this time. In a sense this last is a rather bitter and unbending comment, like the formality of the unintuitive "Thank you" so far. Again the alliteration/assonance of "whole and hale", like the earlier Hopkins-like "Heart had",[143] seems to suggest the breath of the wind or of life, though here it perhaps has a slightly fatuous tone. It is also as if it shows the fracture at this point between her own self after this experience and the former warmth of her relationship to the rest of the warm world, parallel to the way in which she originally would have rejected the austerity of the afternoon and yet took it on. This seems to me the sense of what otherwise looks like a rather cold remove from her dear friend; and it is carried on later in her alteration of the signature (not "I am yours", but "I am"), as if her heart were too occupied to save appearances, and the structure of everything internal and its relationship to this newly discovered, fractured external world were under review.

---

[143] Hopkins (1844–1889) lived in about the same arc of time as she (1830–1886). Cf. for example, a line in "Margaret, are you grieving": "Nor mouth had, no nor mind, expressed / What heart heard of ghost guessed."

But if she in a sense rejects the "New Year" with the bitter image of the fragility and treacherousness of the external state of things, she accepts her friend's "Affection", again a matrix within which it seems possible to assimilate her father's departure. Philosophizing—or perhaps more what Coleridge dubbed "psilosophizing"[144]—about the external world and sense in the ghastly order of things does not help; living the experience with the living does. Even so, the images are strangely detached from a whole person. The metaphor behind "It helps me up the Stairs" (l. 33) is of a supporting arm or hand (again the suggestion of the "Friend" continues). The image of her going "up the Stairs at Night" and glancing at her father's closed door ("Safety itself") is strange. Another aspect of "climbing the Bars of Ecstasy", it seems partly to suggest a child going up, perhaps afraid of the dark and lonely night, glancing at the door to be assured that "there is safety". And yet the image of the "door" is peculiar in itself in the paradoxical way of "We missed him . . .", as if it partly would represent the illusion of safety and yet in fact also locked the child out; even like Dickinson looking on now at the image of her father's dead body behind the prison Bars, where, though he is dead, he is safe, so long as the bars do not lift and he perhaps escape forever. Of course, it may contain the image of the seeds of her foreknowledge as a child; and the interrogative structure would suggest a similar ambiguity ("where . . . was safety", l. 35)—a device she developed to a fine art.[145] The image that takes over from the austere Afternoon of the beginning also seems to suggest her growing older towards death and the 'long sleep' herself; and as such, may be deeply ironical in the observation that, as she did this, she located a point of safety, which also now has been taken away from her. No wing. No keel. So her father's door after his death becomes the opposite of safety, becomes the knowledge of death. There is a poignant, even mathematical beauty in the paradox and its simultaneous containment in the words, where perhaps we are witnessing, in her effort to

[144] "Psilos"-sophizing: bare of wisdom. See, e.g., *Notebooks*, III, 3935.

[145] See above: "Has he no other Realm" in elaboration of quatrain. Also "Did I smile" in "My Life had stood—a Loaded Gun" (P754). It may owe something to the rhetorical Biblical structure—for example, I *Corinthians*, 13:1: "but then shall I know even as also I am known". Again, the three steps leading up to the Calvary cross ghost these images.

transformation of the symbol of "[her] Father's Door", the seed of what was to become the infrastructure of her evolved concept of "Insecurity": "Joy's insuring quality". (Coleridge investigated it using the term "Inconstancy", *Noteboooks*, III, 3562.)

In the last sentence, this suggestion of the detached hand emerges explicitly (linked to the "writing on the wall", *Daniel*, 5:5, perhaps?). It seems the nearest she gets to the "Friend" and the ordinary social world in this letter, in the aftermath of the fracture that needs mending from within. It is worth thinking of this farewell in the context of its factual reference: that is, she never went to her father's grave, as far as we know. One wonders whether this was because she did not want to admit that he was dead and wanted to retain the face, as it were, or because she did not believe in holding on to the old form that keeping a grave might represent (the face must be recuperated within, sought in the stars?). Like the true and false meetings and the flood that falls if it does not rise, the two are eternally possible, but I suggest that what she is working towards, or attempting, is the latter, what she *thought* most truthful, was the latter. She could not visit the grave, but she could accept the friend's Hand (a prophetic hand, like the Christlike figure or the Word that shows and shapes the future) that brought her the clover from it. She could not hang on to her father's old form, but she could accept what forms of him there were in the living, and the former would probably preclude the latter. It is also interesting that it comes at the end of the letter, it seems to me, after the working-out of the death mask (even though as metaphor, the Word, this goes on in her work to elaborate a container for immortality), and the relinquishing of it for an attempt to understand the mystery. As if then only it became possible to thank her friend for a gesture that might otherwise be dangerously ambiguous: not on Mrs Holland's part, but to Emily Dickinson's "internal difference[s]", and to ours, as we attempt to understand her making them.

The structure is also telling. "I seek" looks back to "the Hand"—her friend's, but also God's Hand, as we said, in its impersonality and relation to the "hand lightly created" instructed by "it" and moving in "its" image, as it were. Thus it links to the equivocal austerity of the opening and suggests "I seek its affectonate support", as well as "I seek to face the austere truth" (by means of this handwriting on the wall), and so tenders a link between the Friend and the judge, "if possible" (L381). It also stands intransitive: "I seek, and am Emily", as if the seeking, and her identity—the being-what-she-is—were related, reciprocally essential (as Keats also believed); the "seeking" suggesting the poetic work going on in recuperating the face and understanding ("fixing", as she termed it, L251) the experience. The absence of the conventional "Yours" in the farewell (though she never signed a letter conventionally, as far as I can see) again may suggest her at least temporary separateness from a contractual social world and total immersion in a world of meanings and the search for truthfulness. As I said, the "Hand" suggests God, and the stridency of the statement "I seek, and am Emily" in this case seems to suggest her boldness before God, as if to say: "Well I seek to understand this austerity/what 'Redemption' is, but I am Emily, and meet it only where I find it true, not on compromised ground". And one is reminded of her comment on George Eliot: "The gift of belief which her greatness denied her, I trust she receives in the childhood of the kingdom of Heaven" (L299). The "plucking the clover" (l. 35, perhaps a pun on "lover"), seems to me to confirm this suggestion of God behind the "Hand"-as-plucker-and-plunderer. Take, for example, the image of the Hand in "Except for it's marauding Hand / It had been Heaven below"; or the metaphor for her mother's death later: "Plundered of her dear face . . ." (L371; L782). Of course, this is again the other aspect of the "hand lightly created" in the image of God: the "gun-letter" writer, as it were.

So that in a sense, although in the words of the letter Emily Dickinson has addressed Mrs Holland as a social figure or externally very little, she has evidently used the atmosphere of her affection, the "melodious moment" of her friendship and the congruence Mrs Holland must have had with an internal image or "fiction/Dream" of a true friend, to be able to explore with rigorous words the significance of the loss of her father. "'Kingsley' rejoins 'Argemone'", "Dust unto the Dust", the father seeks the mother, and the author seeks the "fictions" by whom she is created.

4. Conclusion

My aim in Sections II.1–II.3 has been to try to understand something of the development of thought and technique in Emily Dickinson's poetic language; and with this also to suggest how a study of this development in letters dated with certainty might show a method for the internal dating of the poems, as corroboration for, or in contradiction with, the external dating that has already been carried out and the intuitive assumptions made by students of Dickinson's verse poems.

I would, then, briefly like to attempt a paradigm of the developments we have seen in the language and thought. I think it has become clear that these are inextricable, and, to make the problem worse, the 'parts' of language, as the 'parts' of thought and conjoined feeling, when these have meaning, are also inextricable in fact. But we must "try it". And, as I said before, it is my view that an extensive research into the letters using this method should enable us to understand the aesthetic development of the poems; and seen in the light of the tradition of critical terminology it may help us to understand Emily Dickinson's position in relation to the great tradition of the literature in the English language.

As her work develops, the words (her "Icebergs") of her vocabulary expand and find new meanings in new contexts—not only the cardinal words of the Christian religion and literature, but also other, less worn words.[146] She came gradually to invent her

---

[146] See, for example, Sewall's (*Life*, 476) remarking on Dickinson's affection for an impossibly slushy poem by John Pierpont: "One of the mysteries of Emily Dickinson, from our point of view, is how she could enjoy such stuff and yet write the way she did". And elsewhere (ibid., 671/672): "She read hungrily, uncritically, and with her whole being. . . . Her capacity for absorbing what we would consider banalities was apparently lifelong, not just an aberration of youth". Ruth Miller (*Miller*, Appendix III, 403) chides scholars' limited and limiting requirement that great poets should only be influenced by great poets. More specifically, I. A. Richards described many nineteenth-century poets as "critically sensitive people" who yet could not write poetry: "They admired the poetry of previous generations, very rightly, for the taste it left in the head, and failing to realize that the process of putting such a taste into a reader's head involves a great deal of work which does not feel like a

own words, if necessary, from the roots of others and from the images of external objects/occurrences; and increasingly reached back into the "fundamental" histories of words and their compounds, projecting these into the future as she discovered their potential, their new or 'resurrected' meanings. And this possibility was often realized by her development of "unapprehended combinations" (Shelley, "*Defence of Poetry*") of words, both abstract and concrete, or abstract and concrete together, by the dislocation of common idioms and images and by forcing words up against each other to create ambiguity in the paradox between lexical meanings. As this happened, she seems also to have selected a particular vocabulary and to have developed networks of broadening metaphor (often from images/forms of syntax she had used ineffectively earlier) whose "momentous" expansion, however, seems to have created greater "defining" precision (L969) in the thought with which it experimented and which it "fixed" (L251). She gradually loaded certain words with the quality of a symbol, in the original sense of its containing "many-things-thrown-together", and more specifically, I believe, in Coleridge's sense of it "partaking of the Reality which it renders intelligible and, while enunciating the whole, abiding itself as a living part in that Unity, of which it is the representative".[147] But she was not a "symbolist" and, enquiring equally into the nature of the object, of the word, and of their relationship to one another, conversely let her object also contain many words (Emily is Aunt, Uncle, Best little girl; flowers are saints; her dead father is a Star, an Asterisk, and so on). The "Word" was not an empty thing apart bearing relationship only to other empty things, but became deeply integrated with reality. She would not say, I think, with certain writers: "these are just word operations".[148]

She seems to have tried in miniature various modes of writing and to have become able to move rapidly between them according

---

taste in the head while it is being done, attempting therefore to conceive a taste in the head and put it straight on to their paper, they produced tastes in the head which were in fact blurred, complacent and unpleasing" (*Practical Criticsm*, 17).

[147] *The Statesman's Manual*, 30–31.

[148] Iris Murdoch, British TV interview, 1980s.

to her need: between the plane of abstract language used abstractly and that used allegorically, for example; between dramatic speech and bursts of rhapsodic narrative; between the verse-poetic and the prose-poetic. And it is certainly worth considering the validity of her letters as literature/aesthetic objects in the light of this great, functional versatility in her writing.[149]

As far as grammatical syntax is concerned, the study showed her move from those long, accurately grammatical sentences that moved on the surface of things, through a period of violent upheaval, to then gather force into a less fragmented, more pressurized syntax, whose "Piers" are so "brittle" as to seem apparitional, but whose components by then had such "mighty membranes" (L951) that they positively shook with possibility in their concise relation to each other.[150] Throwing into question the reality of our concepts of 'time' and 'space', she came to use tenses to suggest ambiguity or multiplicity of meaning; she used the subjunctive mood to command, to wish in ambiguous contexts; to fix the unity of now and forever in the realm of meaning. She used the indicative where we expect the subjunctive. She developed a tech-

---

[149] Cf. again Langer, *Philosophy* (93, 260): "An idea that contains too many minute yet closely related parts, too many relations within relations, cannot be 'projected' into discursive form; it is too subtle for speech. . . . [the import of the verbal artistic symbol] is not the literal assertion made in the words, but *the way the assertion is made,* and this involves the sound, the tempo, the aura of associations of the words, the long or short sequences of ideas, the wealth or poverty of transient imagery that contains them, the sudden arrest of fantasy by pure fact, or of familiar fact by sudden fantasy, the suspense of literal meaning by a sustained ambiguity resolved in a long-awaited key word, and the unifying, all-embracing artifice of rhythm."

[150] In this context it is difficult not to recall Coleridge's description of "one excellence of the Doctrine of Plato . . . it never suffers its Disciples to forget themselves, lost and scattered in sensible Objects disjoined or *as* disjoined from themselves. . . . It is impossible to understand the elements of the Philosophy without an appeal, at every step and round of the Ladder, to the fact within, to the mind's Consciousness—and in addition to this, instead of lulling the Soul into an indolence of mere attention . . . rouses it to acts and energies of creative Thought, & Recognition—of conscious re-production of states of Being" (*Notebooks,* III, 3935). Richard Holmes' observations (*Early Visions,* 12–13) on the "'architectural' structure of [Coleridge's] prose books" provide interesting reflection on this issue.

nique of ambiguity with the interrogative form in a subordinate clause, also recalling the rhetorical style of the Bible.

As she developed, however, her echoes of Biblical and literary sources grew from being purely imitative, easy to locate in their self-consciousness, and flatly meaningless. They became deeply integrated into her own language, "fundamental" (L898)—that is, not following dead writers' modes, but absorbing their spirit into another one and taking up their arguments, also their "crosses"; not looking for literary status in her quotations from famous—or other—writers, but looking *into their words*, "seeking what [they] mean" (L815); and making them live on or evolve essentially, in "possible" form. It seems clear now that though she was hungry to be published when she was young, as she grew older (and, as Helen Hunt Jackson knew, her work became more necessary to us),[151] the idea came to fairly disgust her. And in an age of the giddy expansion of technological means for communication, hungry for 'great' men, heroic figures, and competitive status, she refused what seemed to her the betrayal of the true spirit of the continuing poetic effort of mankind. For this reason, it is absurd to sustain any view that presents her as refusing the world.

As she worked on the "Icebergs" and their relationship to fact and truth and cast about for different modes in her writing, poetic devices moved into her syntax—alliteration, assonance, rhyme of different sorts, also creating and tapping into new sources of metre. And round about these fell the incidental elements of punctuation and emphasis—the famous dashes, the commas, the underlining (or rather its omission) and capitalization. None of these are used rigidly, but appropriately, in different periods and contexts. Briefly, the dash (like the capital letter, a common feature in nineteenth-century writing in any case) developed from being nothing in particular to creating gaps of pressure, suggestion, and re-formation of meaning, as discussed in Section II.2, to being the pivot of ambiguity between juxtaposed words and clauses, or the creator of a sense of physical gesture in the language. The comma grew in significance as, rather than just to signal the conventional

[151] L937a: "what portfolios of verse you must have. It is a cruel wrong to your 'day and generation' that you will not give them light . . . I do not think we have a right to withhold from the world a word or a thought any more than a *deed*, which might help a single soul."

elements of syntax, it became more used to make emphatic rhythmic pauses or (omitted where expected, as in "The Dust like the Mosquito") "gaps-of-pauses". And the capital became more specific in its context, though again with no absolute rigidity. You will find "Circumference" and "circumference", "One" and "one", according to its context: the "momentous" words are sometimes capitalized, sometimes not; as are the pompous ones that she is criticizing.[152] Heavy underlining in earlier letters mostly disappears, the force of the words later being distributed into other aspects of form capable of more precision and complexity.

Within these changes that force the forms of language to more economy and particularity, to elicit and investigate meanings, she seemed to move from running adrift in a sea of wordy grievance about the loss and autonomy of her friends and the "impregnable chances" of life to an enquiry into the nature of communication between beings. How can you tell whether you can see into somebody's heart or show your own true heart, know "as also [you] are known"? What can words really show you? What relationship do words have to their objects? Can the relationship of one form of words to an object be truer/falser than another? What can you ever really *know* of your object? What can you *know* of your self? This enquiry seems to have involved an experience and recognition of her intense disappointment in people's capacity to communicate, even when they love one another: "How little of our depth we tell, though we confide our shallowness to 'every passing Breeze'—" (L955). And it seems to have sent her inwards to seek to discover in metaphor how to build a true relationship to the world and how to deal with the problem of this being reciprocated, or not. This search, exclusively in words that she could

---

[152] Higginson sustained that Dickinson "followed the Old English and present German method of thus [by capitals] distinguishing every noun substantive" ("Emily Dickinson's Letters" [October 1891], *Atlantic Monthly*, vol. LXVIII). Though nothing so rigidly schematic was the case, it is interesting that he considers she had some acquaintance with these languages. Sewall reports Joseph Lyman's recounting how Dickinson and he read German plays together in the original, with a dictionary to hand (*Life*, 423); and among the books inscribed to Dickinson found in her home, and now in the Houghton Library, appears H. G. Ollendorff's *New Method of Learning to Read German* (1846; see *Miller*, Appendix III, 385). Coleridge's description of "punctuation" as "not symbols of Logic, but dramatic directions, enabling the reader more easily to place himself in the state of the writer or original Speaker" (*Notebooks*, III, 3504) seems helpful to me regarding Dickinson's technique.

"hold" (L330) and that, indeed, could hold her, then took her into the third phase, the answer, as it were, to the questions raised in the 1861 letter: and that is, that we discover our object *in its loss,* in its "escape", because it is then that we most seek to know it, that the Poet most seeks the "Word" for it. The poet exchanges the "squandering" of love in words for the "Rigor" of poetic words, to explore her relationship to all things, to seek the truth—even the bitter truth—of her feeling and their meaning. For it is only thus that we may become "worthy of what we lose" (L765) and make its "discovery" (L535).

Proposal for a type of PERIODIC TABLE

		1851 ltr.	1861 ltr.	1875 itr.
1	Great words of relig. & lit, or common words, forced into new meaning.	—	V	V
2	Invented words.	—	V	V
3	Words reaching back into origins, & projected into future.	—	V	V
4	Unapprehended combinations of words.	—	V	V
5	Transformation of images/common idiom & juxtaposition of words paradoxical to each other, breaking lexical boundaries.	Little	V	V
6	Gradual selecting of vocab/network of metaphors creating form in work, giving lang. "possibility" to mean/Symbolic wds.	Little	V. intense but images disjointed	V intense. Wds & images tied more tightly
7	Variety of modes, register, tone, cohering richness of form of writing.	Little	V	V
8	Grammatical accuracy: (a) tenses (b) moods (c) interrog. clauses.	All accurate, few insig. slips	Significant doubling of tenses	(a) Ambig. use, less obscure. (b) "(other ltr.) (c) "
9	Integration of source into new form & meaning.	Poor	V	V
10	Poetic devices: (a) allit. (b) assonance (c) rhyme (d) metre	—	Little. "Perfect rhyme" poem	a. V b. V c. V
11	Punctuation: (a) dashes (b) comma/full stop (c) underlining (d) capitals	"Normal"—much underlining	Particularized. No underlining	Particularized again but less obscure. No underlining

(The categories are obviously subject to further analysis since this is merely a first attempt at defining them; and should eventually be brought into line with the critical terms of literary tradition.)

Postscript

This work is not complete. Above, a method of close, receptive, and attentive observation and a description of such observation has been applied, in following changes over the years in Dickinson's use of linguistic structures and, within these, also single words. This method has substantial roots in Coleridge: what he described as "steady meditation on the *facts* vitally present and distinctly felt", leading to "the conveyal of Knowledge by words" which "is in direct proportion to the stores and faculties of Observation (internal or external) of the person, who hears or reads them";[153] then in William Empson and I. A. Richards, in the field of literature. Certainly such a method has had wider resonance than only in this field. It finds congruent, progressive formulation, for example, in Donald Meltzer's description regarding psychoanalysis, which could equally well regard poetry:

> there can be little doubt . . . *the foundation of truthfulness [as a mental function] resides in the quality of observation* . . . [Now a *Model* of the Mind—as opposed to a *theory*] of course . . . has

[153] *Notebooks*, III, 3948; 4309, respectively.

> no explanatory power because in psychoanalysis we are working in a non-causal system, where events are factors in a field and everything is symbolic of meaning, metaphorical. For this reason it is essential that models be *used for discovery and not as rules or guides to action*. . . . [It] is essential that it be done by individuals who can think for themselves. This means loneliness, uncertainty, and an inescapable sense of incipient persecution by the group. . . . [But it] is not possible to make observations and find a language for transformations without there being a Model of the World in the back of the mind. *The process of discovery of new phenomena is completely dependent on the explicit and conscious use of a model, in order to recognize the emergence into one's awareness of phenomena which cannot be described by the existing model.* The evolution of the science [I add: of knowledge of the object; for the poet the issue is of her relationship to significant, aesthetic form itself] is of this *inductive–deductive spiral nature,* that *novel phenomena require an extension of the model, and this extension opens to view other phenomena which not only could not be described before, but could not even be recognised.*[154] [my emphases]

There is, in my view, no longer any question that Dickinson's work was in its very essence concerned with the admission, containment, understanding, and transformation of catastrophic experience—not 'catastrophic' in the sense to which we have tended too long and too often to reduce the word—of crippling misfortune and interminable senseless misery; but in that universally vital sense, that Meltzer describes of the "*new idea* . . . [impinging] on the mind *as a catastrophe* for, in order to be assimilated, *[it] sets in flux the entire cognitive structure*" (ibid., 20; my emphasis); Coleridge's "awakening and stepping forward" out of "custom" by means of "Extenders of Consciousness" (*Notebooks,* III, 3632). Bion explored this idea in these terms:

> I suspect there is some counterpart of the term "birth of ideas": that there is some reason to imagine that these painful experiences which we have are related to the process of giving

[154] See *The Apprehension of Beauty: The Role of Aesthetic Conflict in Development, Art and Violence,* Strath Tay, Perthshire, Scotland: Clunie Press, 1988, 203–204.

> birth to an idea—or "struggling to make a connection", which is an instance of thinking. An institution, a society of human beings may be unable to survive the birth pangs of an idea—it splits apart. We are undoubtedly careless with our psychological midwifery. . . . [Bion, 1980, p. 73]

The operation Dickinson effected on her self-in-relation-to-the-outside-world, through language in progressively developed aesthetic form, the procedure she herself investigated and elaborated in her linguistic practice, as in perceiver–perceived relationship, seem to me so congruent to Bion's contemplative description of the (analytic) couple at work, that it may be helpful to quote it at some length:

> . . . We like to feel that we are born and become intelligent and rational human beings , that the "state of mind" when we are awake and conscious is superior to the "state of mind" when we are asleep. We have a prejudice against the other state of mind—that is to say, the one in which we are not. So we try to keep the caesura in good repair . . . to keep our resistance in good working order to act as an impermeable membrane through which thoughts and feelings and ideas of which we have disapproved at one time cannot penetrate. At the same time the thoughts and feelings that we did know at some time still strive to break loose. I could put it like this. We are all bad analysts, but every bad analyst has a good analyst inside him struggling to break free—and we hate it. We say "My God, I'm having a breakdown!" . . . The individual is frightened of even permitting the existence of speculative imaginations of his own; he is afraid of what would happen if anybody else noticed those imaginative speculations, and tried to get rid of him on the grounds of his being a disturbing influence. . . .
>
> . . . I want to suggest that we do not in fact see or observe what we ordinarily think of as "facts". At first the analyst is ignorant of what is happening; if we are honest we have to admit we haven't the faintest idea of what is going on . . . what is our interpretation of the facts which our senses are making available to us? . . . How does the fact—if it is a fact—come over to us who are observing the person? In addition to the evidence which our senses give us there is the evidence which is brought to us not by our sight, but by our *insight*. That is another "fiction". So I want to introduce—borrowing from

> Kant—the idea of *rational conjecture.* I want also to add to that *imaginative conjecture.* When we are waiting for this pattern to emerge we should also be sensitive to our imaginative conjectures and our rational conjectures as a part of the pattern which will perhaps become clearer to a point where we could translate it into words which we would try to communicate. . . .
>
> . . . The truth. What does it look like? Who wants to be confronted with a "trompe l'oeil" representation of Paradise? Such confections are pardonable to an agent selling us our earthly home, but not for our eternal home—our Self. In every job the first stage is an imaginative conjecture. . . . In analysis one's first guess as to what the patient wants could be replaced by something which could be drafted on a piece of paper. Ask yourself what these various stages are before you would be prepared to turn these conjectures into a picture in your own mind. . . . I find it useful to consider that the stages are an imaginative conjecture, a rational conjecture, a pictorial image—the sort of thing you can see in dreams and even "paint" in a verbal version of a pictorial image . . . as if you were engaged on a work of art. . . . [ibid., 28–29, 79, 127, respectively]

A straightforward list of points of contact in progression could helpfully be posited as follows:

Dickinson's recognition of the importance, and indeed her enactment, of keeping open a door to that "other state of mind" can be seen in her images on troubled attention/inspiration:

L190: Strange blooms arise on many stalks and trees receive their tenants. I wish you saw what I can see, and imbibe this music;
The day went down, long time ago, and still a simple choir bear the canto on.
I don't know who it is, that sings, nor *did* I, would I tell;

L265: And when far afterward—a sudden light on Orchards, or a new fashion in the wind troubled my attention—I felt a palsy, here—the Verses just relieve—

L319: the "infinite Beauty" of which you speak comes too near to seek. To escape enchantment, one must always flee.

Her attempts to *not* "keep the caesura in good repair", to have no "impermeable membrane" against "thoughts and feelings and ideas"—for she "believed the love of God may be taught not to seem like bears" (L230)—can be seen in comments such as the famous:

L35: I have heeded beautiful tempters ["builded beautiful temples"—is the difference so great? knowing her, it could even be a syntagmatic pun, and "graphic transactions" were part of her armoury] yet do not think I am wrong;

L42: If we can get our *hearts* "under" I dont have much to fear—I've got all but *three* feelings down, . . . found Father in great agitation at my protracted stay [out]—and mother and Vinnie in tears, for fear that he would kill me;

L403: Be sure to live in vain;

L717: never grow up, which is "far better"— . . . never "improve";

L1037: Not to outgrow Genesis, is a sweet monition;

PF36: How invaluable to be ignorant. . . .

Her awareness of the multiplicious dangers of this operation, external and internal, and her quite staggering, imperturbable determination to go through with it ("You asked would I remain? Irrevocably. . . . I know no other way", L874), can be seen everywhere, and at all times: the danger of being excommunicated as immoral or mad or childish—or "Ought"—by the 'community'; the danger of not being able to stand the entering of knowledge herself; the danger of not being able to bear either her love for the object not being reciprocated, or to bear the (other) possibility of attaining then (certainly) parting from/losing the object; the danger of the desperation at the discovery of the nature of her own attacks on the object in the face of this impotence:

L185: Pardon my sanity;

L209: *Bliss* is unnatural. . . . Insanity to the sane seems so unnecessary—but I am only one, and they are "four and forty", which little affair of numbers leaves me impotent. . . . I am pleasantly located in the deep sea, but love will row you out if her hands are strong, and don't wait till I land, for I'm going ashore on the other side—;

L248: How the sailor strains, when the boat is fillling . . . open your life wide, and take me in;

L268: Perhaps you smile at me. I could not stop for that;

L298: 'Tis dangerous to value, for only the precious can alarm;

L492: Had we the first intimation of the Definition of Life, the calmest of us would be Lunatics!

PF87: It is essential to the sanity of mankind that each one should think the other crazy—a condition with which the Cynicism of Human nature so cordially (readily) complies, one could wish it were a concurrence more noble;

The (perhaps unsent) "Master" letters are particularly demonstrative, I think, of her courage in really experiencing this problem to the depths: indeed, "The Battles of those we love are often unseen" (L895). This is what Coleridge confided to his intimate "Memorandum Books": the "pain of being unintelligible" (*Notebooks*, III, 4182).

The phase of actually entering the attempt—"what is happening", rendered idiosyncratically by her with a sort of present subjunctive: "be" (L233, P516)—when perceiver–perceived really approach and engage with one another, creating storm and uncertainty and awareness of unknowing, can be seen in her comments about "buffeting the sea . . . loving the danger" (L39), "To multiply the Harbors does not reduce the Sea" (L386). This gradually led more and more into her tolerance of her own pain, and to the *freeing*, in a highly complex sense,[155] of her concern and care for the object:

L306: Let me go first, Sue, because I live in the Sea always and know the Road;

L311: Sharper than dying is the death for the dying's sake;

[155] See the way Wilkinson and Willoughby elaborate the infrastructure of this word and use it after Schiller, in their Introduction to their edition of his *Aesthetic Letters* (note 14 above), *passim*.

L332: Dying is a wild Night and a new Road;

L338: There are no dead Katie, the grave is but our moan for them;

L370: Only Love can wound—
Only Love can assist the Wound.
Worthier let us be of this Ample Creature;

L501: Sorrow is unsafe when it is real sorrow. I am glad so many are counterfeits—guileless because they believe themselves;

L671: The little Furniture of Loss has Lips of Dirk to stab us—I hope Heaven is warm—There are so many Barefoot ones;

L1024: Emerging from an Abyss, and reentering it—that is Life; is it not, Dear?

PF70: Death being the first form of Life which we have had the power to Contemplate, our entrance here being an Exclusion from comprehension, it is amazing that the fascination of our predicament does not entice us more. . . .

This then led, I believe, in an analogous progression to that in Bion's description, into the attempt to contain the renewed chaos of actually feeling, and led into imaginative and rational conjecture regarding the event's composition and significance, to contain the disparate elements of the event for the sake of investigating their interrelations. By what means? By bringing to bear what seem congruent holding names (sometimes "the old words are *numb* and there *a'nt* any *new* ones", L252; & Coleridge: "[if] there . . . does not exist a term in our present stock of words significant [of the *fact* or truth which is the premise] . . . a word must be made", *Notebooks*, III, 4309),[156] to prevent the dispersion of the phenomena that "present", in part through our senses:

---

[156] See also Anna Baruzzi: "Emotional awareness depends on the possibility of abstracting particular sensory data from all the elements present in a realisation which successively emerge as being linked by virtue of constant conjunction. These elements, with their relative sensory data, can be considered

L262: Not to see what we love, is very terrible . . .—and nothing does—but just itself ;

L388 Each of us gives or takes heaven in corporeal form, for each of us has the skill of Life;

L410: Thank you . . . for the sweet remembrance. . . . Be sure it was pondered with loving thoughts not unmixed with palates. . . .

L626: Art has a "Palate" as well as an Easel;
The Eyes and Hair—we chose—are all there are . . . ;

L678: I trust we are grateful for the Life that sees—and steps—and touches;

L1025: The Supper was delicate and strange. I ate it with compunction as I would eat a Vision;

but in part through "insight", another "fiction"; and indeed I believe this was the conceptual content of Dickinson's mature use of the word "fiction":

L266: things swell, by leaving, if big in themselves;

L353: [Those loved and lost to us] harrow like a sunset, prooved but not obtained;

L359: Each expiring Secret leaves an Heir, distracting still;

L379: Longing it may be, is the gift no other gift supplies;

---

as abstractions from the overall unity of the elements that constitute the realisation. A second abstraction is then obtained on the assigning of a name, which last is to be understood as something distinct from the realisation that it designates . . . Words are names of various hypotheses on the constant conjunction between certain data. The name given to an object is genetically connected to a selected fact . . . The term is employed for the purpose of avoiding the dispersion of the phenomena, and the rest of the story . . . can be dedicated to determining what it means. §The name is an invention that makes it possible to think and talk about a thing before one knows what it is. §The term is created because the phenomena are without meaning and must be linked together so that they can be thought about." ("Bion on Self-expression" [trans. Morag Harris] *Rivista di Psicoanalisi*, Anno XXVII, n.1, Gennaio–Marzo 1981, Il Pensiero Scientifico Editore, Rome, 640–650; henceforth *Bion*).

L471: the unknown is the largest need of the intellect, though for it, no one thinks to thank God. . . . Without any body, I keep thinking. What kind can that be?;

L587: To the faithful, absence is condensed presence;

L685: the inferential Knowledge—the distinctest one;

L804: your Gifts are from the Sky, more precious than the Birds, because more disembodied;

L989: We dare not trust ourselves to *know* that you have indeed left us. The Fiction is sufficient pain. . . . Ecstasy is peril;

This moment of emotional transition is particularly delicate; a port must be 'in sight' in some way; for the confusion—the "new idea"/idea's birth pang—dissolves the former constellation of the faculties, to make them available to reformation as they accommodate experience:

L522: Danger is not at first, for then we are unconscious, but in the after—slower—Days—Do not try to be saved—but let Redemption find you—as it certainly will—Love is it's own rescue;

L536: no moment must be lost when a heart is breaking, for though it broke so long, each time is newer than the last, if it broke truly;

Words have to be held in check temporarily, as it were, as this process and quest for truthful knowledge—a kind of 'love', exploratory conjoining of perceiver and perceived—gets under way and becomes intensely felt and available for conjecture:

L413 The broadest words are so narrow we can easily cross them—but there is water deeper than those which has no Bridge;

L417: I believe that the sweetest thanks are inaudible. They occur in the Heart and no other knows them. But as two or three awkward Tears supersede Orations, I will say no more. . . . I shall not need an Intercessor;

L730: One who only said "I am sorry" helped me the most when father ceased—it was too soon for language;

L955: The Thank you in my heart obstructs the Thank you on my lips;

L962: Had we less to say to those we love, perhaps we should say it oftener, but the attempt comes, then it is all over, as is said of the dead . . . indeed with the astounding nearness which a dream brings, I must speak this morning; . . . .

Coleridge, too, was very adamant about the significance of this phase, I think; for example (*Notebooks*, III):

[3588] a *real* [vs. verbal] definition of a thing absolutely *known* is impossible;

[3927] here is no room for arguing; but only to know with truth and plainness what we are . . . when the Will . . . substituting the deep desire to supplicate for that of supplication, better prays oftentimes, than the Understanding with all its rhetoric knows how to do—Yet some outward Words we may use, if they come to us, and if we *can* / I say *can*: because if the Quiet be great, whether the Quiet of Awe or of Joy, we shall hardly be able to speak, without *fear*—and dread of scattering and scaring away the blessedness, which broods upon us.

Contingent to this is his evocation of *quality* of the moment of communion and interpenetration with the object: the "truth" as such is imageless. The poet must not mistake the "fictions" he creates for the thing itself (for perhaps not even "matter has being", *Notebooks*, III, 3370); he can, however, wish and hope to bring appearances as congruently as possible to the "idea" of truth, but always involving "discourse" (*Notebooks*, III, 4005) that is not only "plain and fervent" but also *monitored* (*Notebooks*, III, 3659), "self-regulated" (see note 56 above), interweaving opposing parts:

3705: when the Heart of each ripens in the other's looks within the unburst calix—and fear becomes . . . but a fear of losing Hope in Certainty. . . . "I fear to speak, I fear to hear you speak"—So deeply do I now enjoy your presence, so totally possess you in myself, myself in you—The very sound would break the union, and separate *you me* into you and me;

3370 Love, passionate in its deepest tranquillity . . . my whole frame seems to tremble under its touch and . . . pressure like the string of a Lute—with a sense of vibratory Pain distinct from all other sensations, a Pain that seems to shiver and tremble on the threshold of some Joy, that cannot be entered into while I am embodied—a pain of yearning which all the Pleasure on earth could not induce me to relinquish, even were it in my power—and yet it *is* a pain, an aking that spreads even into the eyes, that have a look as if they were asking (a what and a where) even of Vacancy—yea, even when the Beloved is present, seeming to look thro' her and asking for her very Self within or even beyond her apparent Form;

3725: a harmonious Imagery of Forms distinct on the still substance of one deep Feeling, Love & Joy—A Lake—or if a stream, yet flowing so softly, so unwrinkled, that its flow is *Life* not Change—That state, in which all the individuous nature, the distinction without Division, of a vivid Thought is united with the sense and substance of intensest Reality—;

3915: I most commonly do not see her with imagination—have no visual image / but she is present to me, even as two persons at some small distance in the same dark room/ they know that one is present, & act & feel under that knowledge—

3998: Love! as if it were a sense, a faculty to which there was no corresponding Object!;

3999: a Vortex without a center;

4397: As soon as the human mind is intelligibly addressd by any outward medium, exclusive of articulate Speech, so soon does *Art* commence. . . . The Idea that puts the forms together cannot itself be form—it is above Form, is its Essence, the Universal in the Individual, Individuality itself—the Glance and the Exponent of the indwelling Power.

In Dickinson one finds:

L427: Trifles—like Life—and the Sun, we Acknowledge in Church, but the Love that demeans them, having no Confederate, dies without a Term;

L545: We have no statutes here, but each does as it will, which is the sweetest jurisprudence. . . . Again receive the love which comes without aspect, and without herald goes. . . .

It seems to me this 'hovering' phase (Dickinson's "conjecture and discovery"? L459) may be similar to what Bion is describing in his breakdown of the process of evolving the right symbol: being sensitive to, and conjoining imaginative conjecture and rational conjecture, until an image may become expressed, released for further conjunction with another perceiver, to then "reenter the Abyss", as it were, but perhaps, with some gradual increment of understanding and so tolerance:

L277: I think that what we *know*—we can endure that others doubt, until their faith be riper. And so, dear friend, who knew me, I make no argument—to you;

L342: The incredible never surprises us because it is the incredible;

L381: These Behaviors of the Year hurt almost like Music—shifting when it ease us most;

L656: This is but a fragment, but wholes are not below. . . .

It will be evident that, therefore, this study rejects any idea that Dickinson's work was fragmenting, either within the forms of language, or of language from so-called reality, as Porter has posited. Rather, it was re-making, recuperating, projecting, origin-al. It fundamentally constituted that extraordinarily strenuous and difficult thing: "realization that is separation without destruction of unity":[157] a finer and finer distinguishing of "relations within relations" ("defining"), and an increasing expansion of containing means ("momentous"), greater possibility of forms, refinement

[157] Coleridge, *Notebooks*, III, 4489.

and clarity of the basic concepts: "To include, is to be touchless, for Ourself cannot cease—. . . Noon is Morning's Memoir . . ." (L292); "It is deep to live to experience 'And there was no more Sea'—the Fathom though is a daily one and traversed by the simplest Child" (L683). And like all such things, it was also, indeed, attended by danger, "in all the directions". "Love . . . makes but one mistake, it tells us it is 'rest'—perhaps its toil is rest, but what we have not known we shall know again" (L536). "A World too full of beauty for peace" (L 759). Her work is, therefore, a legacy towards which we have enormous responsibility.

This study, furthermore, takes as a given that when language is used aesthetically, poetically—that is, to *mean*, not to conceal, confound or destroy—there is 'something there' which language serves to discover for us and also to form; and that poetically formed language works back and changes the experience of those who make the effort of receiving it, and passing it on, in a continuum. This is what more recently Hasan has described as "language . . . itself not only [being] a part of experience, but intimately involved in the manner in which we construct and organise experience".[158] It is not, however, a recent idea, for it pervades all Coleridge's work, for one, and it surfaces again in Langer, as when she describes aesthetic forms/life-symbols as enabling us "to formulate our conceptions of feeling and our conceptions of visual, factual, and audible reality together . . . to clarify and organize intuition itself".[159]

So, while it takes for granted, as Coleridge began to theorize, that language imaginatively at work takes on an independent life in some sense,[160] it rejects utterly the idea—as untenable as it was fashionable in the years of structuralist criticism—that there is or

---

[158] *Linguistics, Language, and Verbal Art*, Oxford: Oxford University Press [1985], 1989, v.

[159] Langer, *Feeling*, 409 and 397, respectively, and notes 40 and 41 above. See also Stephenson (*Goethe's Conception*), Preface, and note 56 above.

[160] See, e.g., *Notebooks*, III, 3401; 3762: "words are not mere symbols of things & thoughts, but themselves things—and . . . any harmony in the things symbolized will perforce be presented to us more easily as well as with additional beauty by a correspondent harmony of the Symbols with each other. "; Holmes' biography, *Early Visions*, 218n. See also Baruzzi, *Bion* and note 156 above.

can be some kind of indigenously abyssal gap between language and experience, that language becomes a system as such with 'nothing there' but itself. This seems to be the paralysing trap that areas of linguistic study have fallen into and the sort of problem that, for example, Paul J. Thibault has tried to demonstrate was not the direction of thought of original linguistic theorists.[161]

This study analogously rejects the idea that the individual (artist) has no significance in forcing or eliciting progression in the global system of language, that he or she merely passively taps a source, and his or her individual effort in engagement with that source makes no general difference. There must be a crossing-point somewhere. Otherwise, the aesthetic experience that we must all have had at some stage, and which is arguably the very fount of our being able to sustain consciousness, would not have been testified to in the countless ways it has been throughout history, let alone the extraordinarily expert, articulate, and enlightened accounts of it exposed by philosophers of the calibre of Susanne Langer or the experience of it transmitted by artists like Emily Dickinson.

For this reason, this study insists upon trying to avoid any short-cutting in following through the changes, in relationship internal and external to her work, in Dickinson's linguistic form: "how little instructive any criticism can be that does not enter into minutiae", as Coleridge remarked (*Notebooks*, III, 3970). It equally tries to follow, hand in hand, the development of meaning, as intrinsic in the development of linguistic form. It tries to show that the two are not separate areas or aspects that may deny the existence of, or relationship between, each other. There is no substitute for following through the texts as observantly and as openly as possible, step by step. There can be no leaping into undocumented generalizations and theories without the particularity of these foundation stones being laid bare and kept constantly and honestly within vision. Anyone attempting to learn the growth of meaning in Dickinson's work and held intuitively by the staggering, revelatory, and rational beauty of it is infuriatingly frustrated by having no factual idea of the chronological development of her

---

[161] *Re-reading Saussure: The Dynamics of Signs in Social Life*, London: Routledge, 1997; see e.g. Preface, & *passim*.

work and dangerously at risk of simply making up his/her own fictitious story from bits and pieces, including that familiar one—in various forms of adulation or contempt—that she was mad and her language the comment on it. She was not, and her language is indeed the comment on it. So I make no apology for the length and detail of the exposition of the texts.

Still, the work is not complete. There remains to be attempted the application of these findings to the verse poems, and initially—or perhaps rather, concomitantly—therefore, the construction of a viable working method for such application. This will also entail a review of the tradition of critical terminology and the models available or susceptible to enabling a useful viewpoint of the progression of Dickinson's aesthetic forms.

APPENDIX A

Dickinson and Keats: some notes on influence and affinity

In the Annotated Bibliography of his book, *Emily Dickinson's Reading* (Harvard University Press, Cambridge, MA, 1966) Jack Capps quotes the *Ode on a Grecian Urn* in relation to "I died for Beauty—" (P449). But in fact there are many literal echoes of Keats' work in her words, such as I give below (a), as well as areas where their ideas seem to have touched rather specifically (b), either by chance and the spirit of the age or because she may have read Keats' work and letters. Ruth Miller's Appendix III: "Emily Dickinson's Reading", in her 1968 study (*Miller*), does not give any volume of Keats' work as present in the Dickinson household library. In Joanne Feit Diehl's comparison of Dickinson and Keats in *Dickinson & the Romantic Imagination* she mentions that the Dickinson family certainly owned two anthologies of poems containing some of Keats', and the Northampton Library had an 1848 edition of R. Monckton Milnes' *Life, Letters and Literary Remains of John Keats* (1848). As is well known, Keats was one of the few writers she named as among "[her] Books" in the famous L261 to Higginson.

(a)

L62: "Goodbye, dear Austin, yet why Good bye, are you not with me always—whether I wake or sleep?"; *Ode to a Nightingale.*

L63: "Lo the evening cometh, laden with merrie laugh, and happy conversation, and then the sleep and the dream each of a knight or 'Ladie'—"; *The Eve of St. Agnes*?

L204: "People with Wings at option, look loftily at hands and feet, which induces watchfulness!"; letter to Hessey, 8 October 1818: "The Genius of Poetry must work out its own salvation in a man. It cannot be matured by law and precept, but by sensation and watchfulness in itself—That which is creative must create itself—". This may seem a tenuous link. But it is interesting to see how Keats' words seem to echo Shakespeare in *Antony and Cleopatra,* III. xi. 19–20: "Let that be left / Which leaves itself"—rather beautifully the inverse idea in a mirror sentence; and in *Macbeth,* V. iii. 45–46: "Therein the patient / Must minister to himself", both of which Dickinson quoted, the first (L488) with specific reference to her art, and the second (L332) ostensibly about life and work generally, but also about her art.

L233: "Have you the Heart in your breast—Sir—is it set like mine—a little to the left—has it the misgiving—if it wake in the night—perchance—itself to it—a timbrel—itself to it a tune?"; *Ode on a Grecian Urn.* And again: "then I could play in the woods till Dark—till you take me where Sundown cannot find us—and the true keep coming—till the town is full"; *Ode on a Grecian Urn.*

L278: "It is not dying hurts us so—", P335 "'Tis not that Dying hurts us so—"; *Ode to a Nightingale* ("'Tis not through envy of thy happy lot").

L352: "You ask great questions accidentally. To answer them would be events"; letter to Reynolds, 22 November 1817: "I neer found so many beauties in the sonnets—they seem to be full of fine things said unintentionally—in the intensity of working out conceits".

L359: "I have a fear I did not thank you for the thoughtful candy"; "When I have fears that I may cease to be" (possibly from Donne's "I have a sinne of fear, that when I have spunne / My last thread" in *A Hymne to God the Father*).

L438: "If we die, will you come for us, as you do for Father? 'Not born' yourself, 'to die', you must reverse us all"; *Ode to a Nightingale.*

L535A: "Was it from Heaven, or of Men?"; *Ode on a Grecian Urn.*

L794: "a Book is only the Heart's Portrait—every Page a Pulse"; letter to Reynolds, 3 May 1818: "axioms in philosophy are not axioms until they are proved upon our pulses: We read fine—things but never feel them to thee full until we have gone the same steps as the Author".

L898: "Circumference, thou bride / Of awe,—possessing, thou/ Shalt be possessed by / Every hallowed knight / That dares to covet thee"; *Ode on a Grecian Urn.*

L1018: "Oh had that Keats a Severn!" (referring to Helen Hunt Jackson's death). J. F. Diehl (*Dickinson,* 113, cited in note 69 above), suggested she read of Keats' dying words to Severn in Severn's article: "On the Vicissitudes of Keats' Fame", in the *Atlantic Monthly* of April 1863.

L1034: "'and hops and hops in little journeys'"; as Johnson's note indicates, from *Endymion,* and also quoted in Higginson's essay: "The Life of Birds".

L1040: "I could hardly have thought it possible that the scholarly Stranger to whom my Father introduced me, could have mentioned my Friend, almost itself a Vision, or have still left a Legend to relate his name", *Ode to a Nightingale* ("Vision"), *Ode on a Grecian Urn* ("Legend").

Verso of Fragment 47 (also in L493): "A Field of Stubble—lying sere"; *To Autumn* and possibly also *La Belle Dame Sans Merci*. In fact the word "sere" does not come in *La Belle Dame*—as language it probably owes more directly to Milton (*Lycidas*) and Shakespeare (Sonnet 73, and in this context see also her L73: "sere and yellow leaf"). But the idea of sere-ness, and with this the sound ("sedge is withered", "no birds sing"), certainly does, and may even have been in Keats' mind when one considers how "And no birds sing" re-works "where late the sweet birds sang", and the touching-points of the emotional contexts of this sonnet and ballad. Besides, it seems to me, *To Autumn* and *La Belle Dame Sans Merci* were for Keats himself much more deeply and sensibly linked than the traditional view of these two poems could comprehend (consider, for instance, the ambivalence of the autumnal image: "The squirrel's granary is full / And the harvest's done"; or the way "wailful choir" hearkens through "Bare ruin'd choirs" to "no birds sing"). (See also in this connection M. H. Williams, *Inspiration in Milton and Keats*, London: Macmillan, 1982, 177–182.) If this is true, Dickinson would be forging an imaginative link already very much in the air. *La Belle Dame Sans Merci* may also lie behind her use of "fragrant" in L889: "The little package of Ceylon arrived in fragrant safety"; and L897: "Your account of the Lilies was so fresh I could almost pick them, and the hope to meet them in person, in Autumn, thro' your loving Hand, is a fragrant Future."

Prose Fragment 66: "Let me not thirst with this Hock at my Lip, nor beg, with Domains in my pocket"; *Ode to a Nightingale* (perhaps also Psalm 23).

Among other habits of language, Emily Dickinson may also have developed her predilection for creating poetic ambiguity with unusual compounds of "-less" words after Keats (in turn perhaps after Coleridge, who has a plethora of such coinages), and Milton. See, for example, "pathless" in *Il Penseroso*, ll. 69–70, in the light of C. S. Lewis' discussion of the literary evidence of the changing concept of the universe in *The Discarded Image* (Cambridge: Cambridge University Press, 99–100). (See Sections II.2 and II.3 for her very probable echo of line 8 of *Il Penseroso.*) "Viewless" in the *Ode to a Nightingale* seems to mean "unseeing", "invisible","blinding", giving "Poesy" a very complex quality. Dickinson earlier on uses such adjectives quite conventionally (see letters: ceaseless 13, defenceless 14, cheerless 65); but gradually she develops her own compounds, with which she experiments with increasing frequency (touchless 292, charmless 469, guileless 501, deathless 503, murmurless 560, fathomless 766, 799, helpless of 792, impairless 817, alloyless 913, mindless 919, Spotless 928, trackless 938, rebateless 939, soundlessly 948, boundlessness 952, PF95, forgetless 963, pangless 972).

(b)

This latter area is obviously extremely complex and touches on the whole issue of the truth-value of objective certainty, of demonstrable and undemonstrable 'fact'. J. F. Diehl (*Dickinson*) deals with aspects of it that concern the way Dickinson's being a woman affected her as poet in relation to the Romantic tradition, and this is not my concern here. Below I list what seem to me touching points between distinctive ideas that Keats and Dickinson after him were elaborating:

1. The question of the poet's receptivity and his capacity or compulsion to enter imaginatively into the life of all things, primarily as a means of knowing the world but then also of loving it. See Keats, letter to Woodhouse, 27 October 1818: "As to the poetical character itself . . . it is not itself—it has no self—it enjoys light and shade; it lives in gusto, be it foul or fair, high or low, rich or poor, mean or elevated—It has as much delight in conceiving an Iago as an Imogen. What shocks the virtuous philosopher delights the camelion Poet. . . . It is a wretched thing to confess; but it is a very fact that not one word I ever utter can be taken for granted as an opinion growing out of my identical nature. . . . When I am in a room with people if I ever am free from speculation on creations of my own brain, then not myself goes home to myself: but the identity of everyone in the room begins to press upon me, that I am in a very little time

annihilated. . . . All I hope is that . . . the solitary indifference I feel for applause even from the finest Spirits, will not blunt any acuteness of Vision I may have. I do not think it will—I feel assured I should write from the mere yearning and fondness I have for the Beautiful even if my night's labours should be burnt every morning and not eye ever shine upon them. But even now I am perhaps not speaking from myself but from some character in whose soul I now live"; and Dickinson: L107: "I'm so amused at my own ubiquity that I hardly know what to say, or how to relate the story of the wonderful correspondent. First, I arrive from Amherst, then . . . I'm just from Michigan, and am Mattie and Minnie and Lizzie in wondering breath. . . . One thing is true, Darling, the world will be none the wiser, for Emilie's omnipresence, and two big hearts will beat stouter, as tidings from me come in. I love the opportunity to serve those who are mine". These are, as it were, an idea in its early form, or a description of the early stages of a poetic sensibility and its initial sense of power, not to say omnipotence. Certainly Keats' tone in the above passage is a lot more jaunty than it became after the writing of *The Fall of Hyperion*, when he was to say that "the continued stretch of [his] imagination [had killed him]" (*The Keats Circle: Letters and Papers, 1816–1878*, ed. H. E. Rollins, Cambridge, MA: Harvard University Press, 1965). For Emily Dickinson, too, this idea-in-formation gradually became harnessed into the idea of the search for the beautiful, the search to construct an identity or soul as part of the quest for truth—contrary, in one sense, to the apparent suggestion of characterlessness here. And the sense of omnipotence went out of it as the search set in and the question emerged as to whether she used "it" or "it" used her. See also below, part 7 of this Appendix.

2. The total distrust of propaganda in any form and certainty that it involved a compromise of truthfulness. This included propaganda masquerading as art and beauty, as, for example, clichés or forms of speech and verse that have become meaningless. See Keats' letter to Reynolds, 3 February 1818: "We hate poetry that has a palpable design upon us—and if we do not agree, seems to put its hand in its breeches pocket. . . ." And Dickinson L275:

"How extraordinary that Life's large Population contain so few of power to us—and those—a vivid species—who leave no mode—like Tyrian Dye. . . . Do not defraud These—for Gold may be bought—and Purple—may be bought—but the sale of the Spirit—never did occur".

3. The conviction that it is the quality of our emotional experience, of which our faculty for logical reasoning constitutes only a very small, specialized, and indeed dependent part, that determines our capacity to discover and express the truth. See Keats' letter to Bailey, 22 November 1817: "I am certain of nothing but of the holiness of the Heart's affections & the truth of Imagination—What the Imagination seizes as Beauty must be truth—. . . I have never yet been able to perceive how any thing can be known for truth by consequitive reasoning—". And Dickinson: L273: "Fold your little hands—the heart is the only workman we cannot excuse", and L35: "I have heeded beautiful tempters but do not think I am wrong" (Johnson's reading. See Griffin-Wolff [*Emily Dickinson*, 103], regarding J. Leyda's reading [*Leyda*, I, 173): "I have builded beautiful temples".) Dickinson's insistence on "telling the truth slant" seems to me connected to this. Often in letters she does not answer an enquiry in its own discursive terms but instead goes straight into a metaphor, as it were to convey the relation of her whole self to the whole issue, to change point of view on an issue, and make space for further points of view to enter understanding. For example, the famous L268 to Higginson: "Will you tell me my fault, frankly as to yourself. . . . Men do not call the surgeon, to commend—the Bone, but to set it, Sir and fracture within, is more critical. . . . Perhaps you smile at me. I could not stop for that. . . . An ignorance, not of Customs, but if caught with the Dawn—or the Sunset see me—Myself the only Kangaroo among the Beauty, Sir, if you please, it afflicts me, and I thought that instruction would take it away". The first part of the quotation seems to be an exhortation to truthfulness between herself and Higginson on the grounds that a lie is more harmful than any pain caused by the truth. Then, aware that such a demand is bound to be subject to the attack of cynicism, she stands her ground (the holiness of the Heart's affections), and

then the language breaks out in the image (seized by the Imagination as truthful) conveying her sense of unworthiness in the face of the object-aesthetically-conceived, her affliction. It is as if she were saying something like: "I must tell the truth, which involves not calculating what I have to tell you about myself but showing you what I am—and it is like this (the Kangaroo etc)". Her "instruction" seems to have something of the same quality as Keats' "consequitive reasoning": causally, "if you do a) then b) happens"; and like Keats she seems to be expressing disappointment in it. In a similar vein, both poets used sensuous images and talked of the senses as essentially involved in our emotional/psychic consciousness. See, for example, L432a:"If I read a book (and) it makes my whole body so cold no fire ever can warm me I know that is poetry. . . . These are the only ways I know it. Is there any other way?" But it seems to me mistaken to regard this as an incapacity to think abstractly or intellectually, as Allen Tate seems to do (see his essay "Emily Dickinson", in *Saggi* [trans. Nemi D'Agostino], Rome, Edizioni di Storia e Letteratura, 1957).

4. Linked to the above, the question of being able to enter experience as the ship goes out to sea, without having to "pluck the heart of its mystery", without having to reduce to a mass of false "knowledge", the terror, exhilaration, apathy, and so on, and the kind of knowledge that these might accompany. See Keats' letter to the brother Keatses, December 1817: "Negative Capability, that is when a man is capable of being in uncertainties, Mysteries, doubts, without any irritable reaching after fact and reason . . . with a great poet . . . the sense of Beauty . . . obliterates all consideration". And Dickinson, L492: "There is not so much Life as talk of Life, as a general thing. Had we the first intuition of the Definition of Life, the calmest of us would be Lunatics!", or L471: "the unknown is the largest need of the intellect, though for it, no one thinks to thank God". Here Dickinson's "talk of Life" would be akin to Keats' "reaching after fact and reason", and "Life" would be, approaching the "Definition" that might drive you mad, "being in uncertainties, Mysteries, doubts". Then Keats' "sense of Beauty" is connected to what Dickinson elsewhere calls "faith" ("I think that what we

know—we can endure that others doubt, until their faith be riper", L277), or "joy" ("In insecurity to lie / Is Joy's insuring quality", L558)—the guiding principle that is not established easily nor ever completely stable.

5. The idea of the making of the particular soul or identity became something almost sacred to both poets in connection with the discovery of truth, or becoming true/real/immortal. See Keats' letter to the George Keatses, Feb.–May 1819: "There may be intelligences or sparks of the divinity in millions—but they are not souls till they acquire identities, till each one is personally itself . . .—how then are Souls to be made? . . . How but by the medium of a world like this? . . . I think it a grander system of salvation than the chrystain religion—". And Dickinson, L389: "George Eliot is one. The mysteries of human nature surpass the 'mysteries of redemption', for the infinite we only suppose, while we see the finite". They both seem to set this idea off against an idea of redemption or salvation that would involve being, as it were, fished out of the mire by a *deus ex machina*, returning to the divine on the basis of your hopelessness, and prevenient Grace. Keats defended suffering ("a world like this") on the grounds that in conjunction with thought and feeling it makes your identity, it brings you to the divine. This making is a greater celebration of the divine than to suppose that the only way to deal with pain is eventually to be rescued and kindly get taken elsewhere. Similarly, Dickinson holds up George Eliot's making of herself as more divine than man's certainty about immortality, for the one is a thing, a proof of love (we see the finite), while the other is a "conceited" (L184) assumption.

6. More specifically in relation to words, but still linked to all the above: just as the truth can only be discovered and expressed on the basis of a full experiencing of the world, so what is expressed can only be understood or felt on the basis of a feeling experience. Words are not 'just words', they can contain meaning and are directly related to life. See Keats' well known letter to Reynolds, 3 May 1818: "axioms in philosophy are not axioms until they are proved on our pulses: . . . Until we are sick, we understand not". And Dickinson: "I hope you are safe and

distinguished. Is the latter the former? Experience makes me no reply" (L412); or "Dr. Stearns died homelike, asked Eliza for a saucer of strawberries, which she brought him, but he had no hands. 'In such an hour as ye think not' means something when you try it" (L471). But this contained its opposite: namely, that words could be made to be empty of meaning or to distort the truth (such as the doubt, I think, in Dickinson's mind when she questions the congruence of "safe" and "distinguished"). And when that happens, it takes apparent non-sense to get the substance of truth back into them. Keats, a few lines later in the same passage, plays with a quotation from Byron: "'Knowledge is Sorrow'; and I go on to say that 'sorrow is Wisdom'—and further for aught we can know for certainty: 'Wisdom is folly'". Dickinson plays with words in a similar kind of way time and again. (See, e.g., L190, L690, L715.)

7. Finally, the issue of the shattering effect of the effort of searching for the truth through their art and what it meant as this was realized: "Magic, as it electrifies also makes decrepit" (L622), and Keats' remark (made to Severn accompanying him on his final voyage in Italy) cited in (1).

APPENDIX B

The "Loaded Gun", the "pencil in a hand lightly created", and "it": qualities of creativity

I think one sees the evolution of her very idiomatic use of "it" in action in the enigmatic "My Life had stood—a Loaded Gun" (P754, dated conjecturally 1863).[1] As I have said elsewhere (see "Representations of the Male in the Female Imagina-

[1] Studies of this poem—perhaps more than any other single poem—have proliferated over the last twenty years and include: Cameron, Sharon, "'A Loaded Gun': Dickinson & the Dialectic of Rage", in *PLMA* (1978), New York, 93, 423–437; Mario L. D'Avanzo; Edgar P. Stocker, "Two explications of 'Loaded Gun': First Essay: A Source in Wyatt; Essay No. 2: We Roam in Sovereign Woods", in *Dickinson Studies* (June 1982), 42, 40–50; Paula Bennett, *My Life a Loaded Gun: Dickinson, Plath, Rich and Female Creativity*, Urbana, IL: University of Illinois Press, 1986.; Jeanne Holland, "Emily Dickinson, the Master, and the Loaded Gun: The Violence of Re-Figuration", in *ESQ: A Journal of the American Renaissance* (3rd quart. 1987), 33:3, 137–145; Helmut Bonheim, "Narrative Technique in Emily Dickinson's 'My life had stood a loaded gun'", in *Journal of Narrative Technique*, Ypsilanti MI (Fall 1988), 18:3, 258–268; Raymond P. Tripp, "Spiritual Action in 'My Life had stood—a Loaded Gun—'", in *Papers on Language and Literature*, Edwardsville (Summer 1989), 25:3, 282–303; Albert Gelpi, "Emily Dickinson and the Deerslayer" in ed. Richard P. Sugg, *Jungian Literary Criticism*, Evanston, IL: Northwestern University Press, 1992; Lillian Faderman, "Poem 754: Ambivalent Heterosexuality in 'My Life had stood—a Loaded Gun'", in *Women's Studies* (1989), New York, 16:1–2, 121–125; Ellin Ringler-Henderson, "Poem 754", in *Women's Studies* (1989) New York, 16:1–2, 127–31.

tion: The Brontës and Dickinson", note 21 above), this poem is, I think, fundamentally about Dickinson's preoccupation with the capacity of her art to create, but also to destroy, and the distinction between different qualities of destructiveness with which the artist must come to terms.

[1] My Life had stood—a Loaded Gun
In Corners—till a Day
The Owner passed—identified—
And carried Me away—

[5] And now We roam in Sovereign Woods—
And now We hunt the Doe—
And every time I speak for Him
The Mountains straight reply—

[9] And do I smile, such cordial light
Upon the Valley glow—
It is as a Vesuvian face
Had let its pleasure through—

[13] And when at Night—Our good Day done—
I guard my Master's Head—
'Tis better than the Eider-Duck's
Deep Pillow—to have shared—

[17] To foe of His—I'm deadly foe—
None stir the second time—
On whom I lay a Yellow Eye—
Or an emphatic Thumb—

[21] Though I than He—may longer live
He longer must—than I—
For I have but the power to kill,
Without—the power to die—

And, as I pointed out in 1982 (Unpublished thesis: "A Study of the Development of Thought and Technique in Emily Dickinson's Poetic Language", University of Urbino, Appendix D, ix–xvi), it is certainly connected to L656 (near certain dating: September 1880):

> What is it that instructs a hand lightly created, to impel shapes to eyes at a distance, which for them have the

> whole area of life or of death? Yet not a pencil, in the street but has this awful power, though nobody arrests it. An earnest letter is or should be life-warrant or death-warrant, for what is each instant but a gun, harmless because "unloaded", but that touched "goes off?"

Cynthia Griffin Wolff's discussion of the poem (*Emily Dickinson,* 441–446) is, as usual, very lucid, essential, and helpful. Placing the poem in the historical religious context of "Biblical paradoxes", she identifies the poem's "I" unequivocally with "Death" and the poem's "He" with "Christ"/God, as a "premise"—derived from answering the riddle in the last verse via various Biblical references—for reading the whole poem. But apart from the fact that to me it seems a mistake in method to derive the premises for understanding a poem by unriddling the last verse first independently, it also seems to leave various problems unaccounted for: for example, the "I" seems on one level to be a woman, not just a gun-shooting, explosively 'phallic' male death-figure; the explosiveness seems to be in the I/She–He relationship, intrinsic with sexual nuance of various qualities, not in just one of the figures. Furthermore, the "I" seems in part to be the poet herself (with some reference to Keats' Isabella possessively guarding her decapitated lover's head?), with the "gun" aspect, among other things involving a pun on the name of Emily Dickinson's domineering grandmother, Lucretia Gunn—like her Aunt Libbie, a "male relative on the female side" (L473)—whom Griffin Wolff has brought so forcefully into the picture in her biography.

The poem seems haunted by Keats' *La Belle Dame Sans Merci,* and *Isabella,* with the quality of an allegorical romance, ending in a Sphynx-like riddle (ll. 21–24). It has a superficial story of a Lady and a Knight: the Knight comes by and claims her, and the couple roam in the woods and hunt "the Doe" (deer/dear/Christ-child?). So far it is a fairly conventional, ballad-like story. The incomprehensible begins when she/"I" starts to "speak for him" (couldn't he "speak" for himself?); the apposition in deep metaphor of the "Loaded Gun" thrown at us in the first line begins to make itself felt. And it is as well to put very simple questions to oneself. What is her "speaking"? to whom? why should "mountains" reply, and in what sense *can* they? What is the "cordial light" that fills the

Valley? (It seems to throw back on her deigning to smile/smiling with sadistic relish, in that ambiguous interrogative/emphatic linguistic structure that Dickinson came to exploit—"do I smile"; and so on the bright (orgasmic/triumphant/illuminating?) flash of the gunshot going off; and also perhaps looks forward, in the image of a sun breaking through cloud, to the "Yellow Eye".

Then the poem opens into the first simile. This concludes the whole first section (ll. 1–12) where the images are so closeknit, in some way so primitive in the language, that they seem the objects themselves: "It is as a Vesuvian face / Had let its pleasure through". Cousin to "Master" L233's (1861?) "[Vesuvius . . .] said a syllable . . . and [. . .] Pompei hid forever", it builds up a camouflage of knightly beauty and courtesy, tinged with a little Romantic nature—eliciting the sinister aspect of her "smiling" and "speaking". While the predominant *image* is the Lady ("carried away", l. 4), the predominant speaking *voice* is that of a gun (flaring, exploding, banging). In the second half of the poem, the predominant image becomes the gun, but the voice becomes less steely, more humane—to a concentrated degree so in the final riddle.

The poem then moves into the dark night, with "good day done", possibly a harbinger of 'bad night' as well as a pun on the formality "good day", hardly expressive of intimacy between lovers as they go to bed. There is irony in the representation of the over-good manners of the two: their courtesy seems in part just a masked form of bargaining and playing each other off and walks the usual fine line that subsists between ganglike persecutory collusion against the world and mutual treachery. And by the time one has realized that the image of the gun is taking over in the fourth verse, that "guarding my Master's head" (l. 14) already sounds as if she's murdered him. To limit the significance of the symbolic couple to sign-allegory at this point, only "Death" and "Christ", seems to give very little help in understanding the effort of investigation of qualities of relationship that is being exposed in the poem's progression. It *is*, as Griffin Wolff says, a difficult poem; but, differently from her, I think it is not so much "cryptic" as deeply ambiguous and ambivalent, at grips with some of the most cogent and disturbing issues in the poet's creativity, perhaps in some way connected to a kind of 'baby'-murder, I suggest, in an analogous way to the difficulty of *Lamia* in relation to Keats' overall production. Suddenly in the dark the voice that no longer speaks through the external images visible in the daylight is no longer veiled by them and emerges to show the hardness of its internal nature. It prefers jealously guarding its decapitated Master's Head to "sharing the Eider-Duck's deep Pillow": that is, to being his lover (the shared pillow)/to dying–lying with him where he lies dead ("deep"—below earth; see also "King of Down" in L432 discussed in Section II.3).

But there is also a sense of the identity of the lady and the knight, first anticipated at their meeting in "identified": "recognized as mine/made identical"; plus its grammatical versatility as a past verb–past participle: the owner "identified"/the owner "was identified by" My Life. And this, together with this other—inextricable—sense of their total opposition, antithesis, is continued in the next verse. The shape of "To foe of His—I'm deadly foe" seems both to match foe against foe (the he–she complicity/collusion against the world), but also to match him against her: equally, as the "foe" (l. 17) *is* the "foe", he *is* one with her. "None stir the second time"—the subjunctive/imperative shadowing the plural indicative here ("stir") functioning rather like a spell—picks up the image of his sleeping, even though it also refers to the foe being shot dead. And again, while that "Yellow Eye" and "Emphatic Thumb" are supposedly directed at the foe (strangely non-specific in the external world of the poem, and picking up the rhyming, defenceless, perhaps childlike "Doe" of the first half), they seem directed at him too, because they pick up in a very 'part-object' way, like nothing else here does, the ghost of her human body. That body, which should be lying with the knight, is instead glaring at him and pulling the trigger. And here again she seems identical with him in that gesture—it was he before who pulled it ("I speak *for him*"). As I said before, the "Yellow Eye" is another aspect or more evolved image of the earlier "cordial light". The eye and the hand form one of the links to the letter passage, though they function slightly differently there; but the hand holds the pencil (or is another aspect of what the pencil also 'is', insofar as these are all images for something that we cannot otherwise see) that has that awful power to kill or to bring to light/illuminate, that has direct access to heart-strings ("cordial"), as it were. And here in the poem, too, we seem to stand on a knife-edge between life and death—which is truer, the apparent courtesy or the apparent treachery? Is her smiling a deadly explosion or a communication? Does the good day give way to bad night or 'goodnight'; does she not become his lover because she is guarding him or because she is murdering him?

With these three figures, then—the knight, the lady, and the gun hovering between them as they interrelate in various constellations—we move into the riddle that elicits the growing question more explicitly: "What *are* they?" It seems to bear the same relation to the poem as the "for what is each instant but a gun" solution to the rest of the letter passage. But it is so enigmatic (despite Griffin Wolff's identification of Biblical sources, for these do not tell us what Dickinson *does* with them) that it sends us back over the whole poem anyway. By the poem's riddle, the gun is attached, predominantly, to the "I". Even the eye and thumb it takes on are infused with "gunnishness", and its voice is laid barer than in the first half of the poem. But something different happens in the riddle. She seems to be saying: "*Because I am made of metal that does not turn to dust like human flesh does, I may live longer* (the "may" seems to pick up the imperious aspect of the gun's persona—"I may, if I choose"; and also a more vulnerable human aspect—"there's a possibility that I shall"—just as the Gun/My Life were destitute until the Owner passed). *But he simply must live longer* (again there is both the vulnerability of a plea and the brutality of a command—"O please let him"/ "he will whether he likes it or not"); *because I can kill* (take wonderful trophies in regal places, like the doe–foe in mountainous scenery, if I am carried along by him; but commit shabby little murders if left to myself—standing around in dark corners under the pressure of my own emphatic thumb that perhaps turns against its identical part?). This seems to me similar to the (poet's) pencil that has the awful power to shoot off explosive little messages even if it is not guided by a master, and how terrible that can be—and nobody arrests (puts a stop to) it!/even if nobody should arrest it ('take it up to use it'). (This is an instance where Dickinson exploits mood variation, here using an indicative where one might have expected a subjunctive. She very often exploited the inverse in later work.) *And that is a great power. But I cannot die* (partly, I lack a greater power—"dying", with its traditional punning associations, perhaps being the epitome of human qualities; she may be powerful, but she is not feeling—she can guard her Master's Head, but she cannot share his bed. And this picks up the plea-aspect of "he must live", because He is more humane than "I"; the pencil without the hand is worse than nothing). But another aspect of the statement in its context is the reiteration of the gun's blind force and indestructibility: *my only capacity is to kill; also, I will never die, so if left to myself, I will just stand around neglected in dark corners, potentially murderous to no purpose. I need the Master, to come into the world, and I need the Master (whatever he "is") to go on creating constructively* (killing constructively? it seems to walk a fine line). This seems to me the more humane voice underlying the predominant gun image at the end of the poem. Its brutality is undermined by its ultimate concession of dependence on the knight, indeed its *will* to be dependent, and the implicit praise of humane values. If it is true, as I think, that this poem is an allegorical demonstration of the creative process, it does seem to say that any art, any expression, is in some sense inevitably an act of violation, and, as I said at the beginning, the artist is constrained to distinguish fundamentally between, and come to terms with—perhaps at great cost—different qualities of destructiveness. These seem to me issues currently being investigated very centrally in certain areas of psychoanalysis.

There are many points of contact between the poem and the letter. An important one is, I suggest, the pencil (in reality not divisible from its hand) and the gun (in reality not divisble from the lady). They are both eternal and will outlive the hand that moves them (in their inhuman aspect), and this eternity may be related to the eternity/universality of art. They both create shapes, that eyes outside them (also their own?) see, and these shapes have great beauty or terrible beauty. I refer particularly to the second and third verses of the poem and suggest that there is a parallel between the "eyes that can see at a distance", the massive "whole area of Life or of death", and the seeing the vast mountains, the sun on the valley, and, as it were, Vesuvius' mighty eruption. (She still wrote of "cordial mountains", and "speechless mountains", in L948:1884 and L1000:1885, respectively.) Perhaps in this sense, the moving from the instructed hand (in the prose passage) to the inhuman "pencil" (why not repeat "hand", for example) is a similar technique, or at least a parallel movement in the language, to the poem's oscillating between Gun and Lady—is a description of an inhuman force that 'takes over' (is?) the act of creation or destruction, that can kill or save whoever is at the receiving end (even the hand that makes it "go off"?), and that *does not care,* once the fuse has been lit and the creation is on its way, any more than the event of birth stops because because it 'knows' the mother's—or childs—life may be in danger. But somewhere, both in the poem and the prose, beyond the gun and beyond the pencil (of the artist), there is a force that is 'caring', as it were, about what happens. And it seems to me the caring lies in the ambiguities: for example, in the letter (which was, it is true, probably written 20 years later), while Dickinson is saying that the pencil's power cannot be denied and is eternal, she is also saying, on one level; "Why isn't anybody stopping it?" In the poem, it is the lady's human voice that emerges, to remain, beyond the invincibleness of the gun.

There is also a link between the letter's "unloaded gun" (presumably an "instant" not yet belonging to any body's precise life and so having no specific import), that goes off by being touched by a letter (either creating a letter, a shape; or receiving a letter—the grammar holds both possibilities), and the lady–gun (the loaded life—the instant in a specific context) being touched by her knight, her owner, so that she talks and smiles, "goes off".

What they both, then, seem to be depicting is a creative or destructive force that is objective and autonomous but beecomes harnessed into a hand (the Master—or Lady—of the poem? the letter writer or receiver?) that will use it either to create or destroy, or both perhaps in some more complex constellation; but whatever it does, it does it both to itself and to its object. Still, the event and its determining quality seem to lie in the kind of *relationship* between the parts.

BIBLIOGRAPHY

Alvarez, A. *The Savage God: A Study of Suicide*. Harmondsworth, Middlesex: Penguin, 1971.

Anderson, Charles, *Emily Dickinson's Poetry: Stairway of Surprise*. New York: Holt, Rinehart & Winston, 1960.

Bacigalupo, Massimo (ed.), *Dickinson: Poesie* (especially Introductory sections pp. vii–xliii). Milan: Mondadori, 1995.

Barbot, Mary Elizabeth, "Emily Dickinson Parallels". *New England Quarterly*, XIV (1941), 689–696.

Barfield, Owen, *Poetic Diction*. London: Faber and Faber, 1952 (reissue).

Barfield, Owen, *History in English Words*. London: Faber and Faber, 1956.

Baruzzi, Anna, "Bion on Self-expression". *Rivista di Psicoanalisi*, XXVII, no. 1, January–March 1981, Rome, Il Pensiero Scientifico Editore, 640–650.

Bennett, Paula, *Emily Dickinson: Woman Poet*. Iowa City, IA: University of Iowa Press, 1990.

Bennett, Paula, *My Life a Loaded Gun: Dickinson, Plath, Rich and Female Creativity*. Urbana, IL: University of Illinois Press, 1986.

Bion, Wilfred R., *Bion in New York and São Paolo*, ed. by F. Bion. Perthshire, Scotland: Clunie Press, 1980.

Blackmur, R. P., "Emily Dickinson: Notes on Prejudice and Fact". reprinted in Caesar R. Blake & Carlton F. Wells (eds.), *The Recognition of Emily Dickinson: Selected Criticism since 1890.* Ann Arbor, MI: University of Michigan Press, 1964.

Blake, W., *Complete Writings*, ed. by Geoffrey Keynes. Oxford: Oxford University Press [1966] 1972.

Bonheim, Helmut, "Narrative Technique in Emily Dickinson's 'My life had stood a loaded gun'". *Journal of Narrative Technique*, Ypsilanti MI (Fall 1988), 18, No. 3, 258–268.

Brentano (von Arnim), Bettina (1840), *Correspondence of Fräulein Günderode and Bettina von Arnim* ([1842] trans. by Margaret Fuller), Boston, MA: Burnham, 1860.

Brontë, Charlotte, *Jane Eyre*, 1847.

Brontë, Emily Jane, *The Complete Poems of*, ed. by C. W. Hatfield. New York: Columbia University Press, 1941.

Buell, Lawrence, *Literary Transcendentalism: Style and Vision in the American Renaissance*. Ithaca, NY: Cornell University Press, 1973.

Burnett, A. P., "Pentheus and Dionysus: Host and Guest". *Classical Philology*, 65 (1970), 15–29.

Cambon, Glauco, "Emily Dickinson's Circumference". *Sewanee Review* (1976), TN, 84, 342–350.

Cameron, Sharon, "'A Loaded Gun': Dickinson & the Dialectic of Rage". *PMLA* (1978), New York, 93, 423–437.

Cameron, Sharon, *Lyric Time: Dickinson and the Limits of Genre*. Baltimore & London: The Johns Hopkins University Press, 1981.

Cameron, Sharon, *Choosing Not Choosing: Dickinson's Fascicles*. Chicago, IL & London: University of Chicago Press, 1992.

Cappeluti, J. A. "Fading Ratios: Johnson's Variorum Edition of Emily Dickinson's Poetry". *Emily Dickinson Journal* (1992), Niwot, CO., 1, No. 2, 100–120.

Capps, Jack, *Emily Dickinson's Reading*. Cambridge, MA: Harvard University Press, 1966.

Chase, Richard, *Emily Dickinson*. London: Methuen, 1952.

Chaucer, G., *The Works of*, ed. by F. N. Robinson. London: Oxford University Press, 1957.

Clarke Mossberg, Barbara A., *Emily Dickinson: When a Writer Is a Daughter*. Bloomington, IN: Indiana University Press, 1982.

Cody, John, *After Great Pain: The Inner Life of Emily Dickinson*. Cambridge, MA: Harvard University Press, 1971.

Cook, Carol L., "The Psychic Development of a Woman Writer". *University of Dayton Review* (Winter 1987–1988), Dayton, OH, 19, No. 1, 111–119.

Coleridge, S. T., *Biographia Literaria*, ed. by G. Watson. London: Dent & Dutton, 1975.

Coleridge, S. T., *The Notebooks of* (Text & Notes) (3 vols.), ed. by Kathleen Coburn. London: Routledge and Kegan Paul, 1973.

Coleridge, S. T., *The Statesman's Manual*, 1816, *Lay Sermons*, ed. by R. J. White. London: Routledge and Kegan Paul, 1972.

Coleridge, S. T., *Shakespearean Criticism* (2 vols.), ed. by T. M. Raysor. London: Dent, 1960.

Czerny, Dennis L., "'My Classics Vail Their Faces': Uncovering the Latin and Greek Elements in Emily Dickinson's Poetry". *Dissertation Abstracts International*, Ann Arbor MI (December 1993), 54.

Dandurand, Karen, "Another Dickinson Poem Published in Her Lifetime". *American Literature*, Durham, NC (October 1982), 54, No. 3, 434–437.

Dandurand, Karen, "New Dickinson Civil War Publications", *American Literature* (March 1984), 56, No. 1, 17–27.

D'Avanzo, Mario L.; Edgar P. Stocker, "Two explications of 'Loaded Gun': First Essay: A Source in Wyatt; Essay No. 2: We Roam in Sovereign Woods". *Dickinson Studies*, 42 (June 1982), 40–50.

Decker W. L., "'A Letter Always Seemed to Me Like Immortality': The Correspondence of Emily Dickinson". *ESQ: A Journal of the American Renaissance* (1993), Pullman, WA, 39, No. 2–3, 77–105.

Dickinson, Edward, "Female Education", *New England Inquirer*, January 5, 1827.

Dickinson, Emily, *The Letters of* (3 vols.), ed. by Thomas H. Johnson & Theodora Ward. Cambridge, MA: The Belknap Press of Harvard University Press, 1958.

Dickinson, Emily, *The Poems of* (3 vols., including variant readings criticially compared with all known manuscripts). Cambridge, MA: The Belknap Press of Harvard University Press [1951], 1979.

Dickinson, Emily, *The Complete Poems*, ed. by T. H. Johnson. London: Faber and Faber, 1970.

Dickinson, Emily, *A Concordance to the Poems of Emily Dickinson,* ed. by S. P. Rosenbaum. Ithaca, NY, & London: Cornell University Press, 1964.

Dickinson, Emily, *The Poems of Emily Dickinson: An Annotated Guide,* ed. by J. Duchac. New York: 1979.

Dodds, E. R., *The Greeks and the Irrational.* Berkeley, Los Angeles, CA: University of Los Angeles Press, 1951.

Dodds, E. R., "Euripides the Irrationalist". *Classical Review,* 43 (1929) 97–104; also in *The Ancient Concept of Progress and Other Essays,* Ch. 6. Oxford: Clarendon Press, 1973.

Donne, John, *Complete Verse and Selected Prose.* London: Nonesuch [1929] 1978.

Donoghue, Denis, in: *Six American Poets,* ed. by Allen Tate. Minneapolis, MN: Minnesota University Press, 1969.

Duchac, J. (ed.), *The Poems of Emily Dickinson: An Annotated Guide to Commentary Published in English.* New York: G. K. Hall, 1993.

Emerson, Ralph Waldo, *Complete Works,* ed. A. C. Hearn. Edinburgh: Nimmo, Hay and Mitchell, 1906.

Empson, William, *Seven Types of Ambiguity.* Harmondsworth, Middlesex: Penguin [1930] 1961.

Euripides, *Bacchae,* ed. by E. R. Dodds. Oxford: Clarendon Press, 1960.

Euripides, *Hippolytus,* trans. E. P. Coleridge. London: George Bell & Sons, 1898.

Faderman, Lilian, "Emily Dickinson's Letters to Sue Gilbert". *Massachusetts Review,* 18 (1977), 197–255.

Faderman, Lilian, "Poem 754: Ambivalent Heterosexuality in 'My Life had stood—a Loaded Gun'." *Women's Studies,* New York, 16 (1989), nos. 1–2, 121–125.

Farr, Judith, *The Passion of Emily Dickinson.* Cambridge, MA: Harvard University Press, 1992.

Feit Diehl, Joanne, *Dickinson and the Romantic Imagination.* Princeton, NJ: Princeton University Press, 1981.

Ferlazzo, Paul, *Emily Dickinson.* Boston, MA: Twayne, 1976.

Franklin, Ralph William, *The Editing of Emily Dickinson: A Reconsideration.* Madison, WI: University of Wisconsin Press, 1967.

Franklin, Ralph William (ed.), *The Manuscript Books of Emily Dickinson* (2 vols.). Cambridge, MA: The Belknap Press of Harvard University Press, 1981.

Frye, Northrop, in: Perry Miller et al. (Eds.), *Major Writers of America* (2 vols.). New York: Harcourt, Brace and World, 1962, 2: 10.

Frye, Northrop, *Anatomy of Criticism: Four Essays*. Princeton, NJ: Princeton University Press, 1971.

Gawain poet, *Sir Gawain and the Green Knight* (2nd) ed. by N. Davis. Oxford: Clarendon Press, 1972.

Gelpi, Albert, *The Mind of the Poet*. Cambridge, MA: Harvard University Press, 1965.

Gelpi, Albert, "Emily Dickinson and the Deerslayer". In: Richard P. Sugg (ed.), *Jungian Literary Criticism*. Evanston, IL: Northwestern University Press, 1992.

Gerlach, John, "Reading Dickinson: Bolts, Hounds, the Variorum, and Fascicle 39". *Emily Dickinson Journal* (1994), 3, no. 2, 78–99.

Graves, R. N., "Dickinson's Letters 263 and 271". *Explicator*, Washington, DC, 53, No. 3 (Spring 1995), 152–156.

Griffin Wolff, Cynthia, *Emily Dickinson*. Radcliffe Biography Series. Reading, MA: Addison-Wesley, 1986.

Harris, Morag, "A Study of the Development of Thought and Technique in Emily Dickinson's Poetic Language". Unpublished thesis, University of Urbino (Winter 1982/3).

Harris, Morag, "Emily Dickinson's Search for the Chiefest Words", in *Spicilegio Moderno: Letteratura Lingue Idee*, no. 19/20 (1986). Bologna: Bologna University Journal, Galeati.

Harris, Morag, "Representations of the Male in the Female Imagination: The Brontës and Dickinson", in *Gramma: Journal of Theory and Criticism*, vol. 4. Thessaloniki: Aristotle University Publications (1996), 129–152.

Harris, Morag, "'Myself' and the 'supposed person': Emily Brontë & Dickinson", in R. Baccolini, Carla Comellini, Vita Fortunati (Eds.), *Il Centauro Anglo–Americano: Culture de Lingua Inglese a Confronto* (proceedings of the XVIIth Conference, Italian Association of English Scholars, February 1995). Bologna, CLUEB, July 1998.

Harris, Sharon M. "The 'Cloth of Dreams': Dream Imagery in Dickinson's Poetry and Prose", in *Dickinson Studies*, 68 (1988), 3–16.

Harris Williams, Meg, *Inspiration in Milton and Keats*. London: Macmillan, 1982 [see also: Donald Meltzer; Margot Waddell].

Hart, E. L.,"The Elizabeth Whitney Putnam Manuscripts and New

Strategies for Editing Emily Dickinson's Letters". *Emily Dickinson Journal*, Niwot CO., 4 (1995), no. 1, 44–74.

Hasan, Ruqaiya, *Linguistics, Language, and Verbal Art*. Oxford: Oxford University Press, 1989.

Heginbotham, Eleanor E., "Dwelling in Possibilities: The Fascicles of Emily Dickinson". *Dissertation Abstracts International*, Ann Arbor, MI, 54, no. 1 (July 1993).

Herbert, George, *The English Poems of*, ed. by C. A. Patrides. London: Dent, 1974.

Higginson, T. W. "Ought Women to Learn the Alphabet?" *Atlantic Monthly*, III, no. 15 (February 1859), 137–150.

Higginson, T. W. "Letter to a Young Contributor". *Atlantic Monthly*, IX, no. 54 (April 1862), 401–411.

Higginson, T. W. "Emily Dickinson's Letters". *Atlantic Monthly*, LXVIII (October 1891).

Holland, Jeanne, "Emily Dickinson, the Master, and the Loaded Gun: The Violence of Re-Figuration". *ESQ: A Journal of the American Renaissance*, 33, no. 3 (3rd quart. 1987), 137–145.

Holmes, Richard, *Coleridge, Volume I: Early Visions*. London: Hodder and Stoughton, 1989.

Homans, Margaret, *Woman Writers and Poetic Identity: Dorothy Wordsworth, Emily Brontë, and Emily Dickinson*. Princeton, NJ: Princeton University Press, 1981.

Hopkins, G. M., *The Poems of*, ed. by Gardner & MacKenzie. London: Oxford University Press, 1970.

Hunt Jackson, Helen, in *The Letters of Emily Dickinson* (see "Main Texts above): Letter 937a.

Johnson, Thomas J., *Emily Dickinson: An Interpretive Biography*. Cambridge, MA: The Belknap Press of Harvard University Press, 1955, 967.

James, Alice: see Waggoner, H.

James, Henry, *The Europeans*. Harmondsworth, Middlesex: Penguin, 1964.

Juhasz, Susanne, *The Undiscovered Continent: Emily Dickinson and the Space of the Mind*. Bloomington, IN: Indiana University Press, 1983.

Juhasz, Susanne, "Reading Emily Dickinson's Letters". *ESQ: A Journal of the American Renaissance*, Pullman WA., 30, No. 3 (1984, 3rd Quart.), 170–192.

Keats, John, *A Selection of Letters*, ed. by R. Gittings. London: Oxford University Press, 1975 (reprint).

Keats, John, *The Complete Poems*, ed. by Miriam Allott. London: Longman, 1970 [see also: H. E. Rollins (ed.) below].

Keller, Karl, *The Only Kangaroo Among the Beauty*. Baltimore & London: Johns Hopkins University Press, 1979.

Kirkby, Joan, *Emily Dickinson*. London: Macmillan, 1991.

Kitto, H. D. F., *The Greeks*. Harmondsworth, Middlesex: Penguin [1951] 1963.

Lambert R. G., *A Critical Study of Emily Dickinson's Letters: The Prose of a Poet*. New York: Edwin Mellen Press, 1996.

Langer, Susanne K., *Philosophy in a New Key: A Study in the Symbolism of Reason, Rite, and Art*. Cambridge, MA: Harvard University Press [1942] 1979.

Langer, Susanne K., *Feeling and Form: A Theory of Art*. London: Routledge and Kegan Paul [1953] 1979.

Levi St. Armand, Barton, *Emily Dickinson and Her Culture: The Soul's Society*. Cambridge, UK: Cambridge University Press, 1984.

Lewis, C. S., *The Discarded Image*. Cambridge, UK: Cambridge University Press, 1964.

Lewis, C. S., *Experiment in Criticism*. Cambridge, UK: Cambridge University Press, 1961.

Leyda, Jay, *The Years and Hours of Emily Dickinson* (2 vols.). New Haven, CT: Yale University Press, 1960.

Lindberg-Seyersted, Brita, *The Voice of the Poet: Aspects of Style in the Poetry of Emily Dickinson*, Uppsala: Acta Universitatis Upsaliensis, Studia Anglistica Upsaliensia 6, 1968.

Lilliedahl, Ann, "Emily Dickinson in Europe: Her Reputation in Selected Countries". Washington, DC: University Press of America, 1981.

Loeffelholz, Mary, *Dickinson and the Boundaries of Feminist Theory*. Urbana, IL: University of Illinois Press, 1991.

Loomis Todd, Mabel, from her journal: in R. B. Sewall, *The Life of Emily Dickinson* (see below).

Loeschke, Maravene, "Challenges of Portraying Emily Dickinson's in William Luce's Play 'The Belle of Amherst'". *Emily Dickinson Journal*, Niwot, CO, 2 (1993), no. 2, 124–129.

Lowell, Amy, *Poetry and Poets: Essays*, Boston, 1930.

Lucas, D. D., *Emily Dickinson and Riddle*, Dekalb, IL: Northern Illinois Press, 1969.

Luce, William, *The Belle of Amherst: A Play Based on the Life of Emily Dickinson*. Boston, MA: Houghton Mifflin, 1978.

MacLeish, Archibald, Bogan, Louise, & Wilbur, Richard, *Emily Dickinson: Three Views*, Amherst, MA: Amherst College Press, 1960.

MacLeish, Archibald, Bogan, Louise, & Wilbur, Richard, *Poetry and Experience*. Harmondsworth, Middlesex: Penguin, 1969.

MacNeice, Louis, *Modern Poetry: A Personal Essay*. Oxford: Clarendon Press, 1968.

McLure Mudge, Jean, *Emily Dickinson and the Image of Home*. Amherst, MA: University of Massachusetts Press, 1975.

McKinstry, S. J., "'How Lovely Are the Wiles of Words!—or, 'subjects Hinder Talk': The Letters of Emily Dickinson" in *Engendering the Word: Feminist Essays in Psychosexual Poetics*, ed. & intro. by T. F. Berg, A. S. Elfenebin, J. Larsen, E. K. Sparks; fwd. by S. Gilbert. Urbana, IL: University of Illinois Press, 1989.

McNeil, Helen, *Emily Dickinson*. London: Virago Press, 1986.

Meltzer, Donald, "The Interaction of Visual and Verbal Language in Dreams", in *Essays in Honor of Arthur J. Bronstein*. New York: Raphael, 1983.

Meltzer, Donald, & Harris Williams, Meg, *The Apprehension of Beauty: The Role of Aesthetic Conflict in Development, Art and Violence*. Perthshire, Scotland: Clunie Press, 1988.

Miller, Ruth, *The Poetry of Emily Dickinson*. Middletown, CT: Wesleyan University Press, 1968.

Milton, John, *Complete Shorter Poems of*, ed. by J. Carey. London: Longman, 1977.

Milton, John, *Paradise Lost*, ed. by A. Fowler. London: Longman, 1974.

Milton, John, *Areopagitica*, ed. by K. M. Lea. Oxford: 1973.

Money-Kyrle, Roger, *The Collected Papers of*, ed. by Donald Meltzer & Edna O'Shaughnessy. Perthshire, Scotland: Clunie Press, 1978.

Monckton Milnes, R., *Life, Letters and Literary Remains of John Keats*. New York: Putnam, 1848.

Monteiro, G. *Facsimile Poems: 1890, 1891, 1896 editions*. Gainsville, Florida Scholars' Facsimiles & Reprints, 1967.

Moore, Marianne, "Review of Emily Dickinson's Letters". *Poetry*, Chicago, 41 (January 1933), 219–226.

Morey, Frederick L., "Dickinson–Kant: The First Critique". *Dickinson Studies*, Washington, DC, 64 (1987), 3–30.

Morey, Frederick L., "Dickinson–Kant, II (covering the second critique, that of Practical Reason)". *Dickinson Studies*, Washington, DC, 64 (1987), 3–30.

Morey, Frederick L., "Dickinson–Kant, III: The Beautiful and the Sublime" in *Dickinson Studies*, Washington, DC, 67 (1988), 3–60.

Morey, Frederick L., "Dickinson–Kant, IV", in *Dickinson Studies*, Washington, DC, 74 (1990), 1–61.

Morisco, Gabriella, "Emily Dickinson: Transgressing and Transcending the Nineties", in Nicole Rowan (ed.), *(W)righting the Nineties: Proceedings of the ERASMUS Conference May 1994*. Ghent, English Department University of Ghent, 1995, 29–50.

Morisco, Gabriella, "Emily Dickinson: Witchcraft Has Not A Pedigree", in A. Usandizaga & E. Russell (Eds.), *Wayward Girls and Wicked Women*: In Memoriam of Angela Carter. Bellaterra, Departament de Filologia Anglesa i de Germanistica, Università Autònoma de Barcelona, 1995.

Morris, Timothy, "The Development of Dickinson's Style". *American Literature*, Durham NC, 60, NO. 1 (March 1988), 26–41.

Nath Ker, Inder, *The Landscape of Absence: Emily Dickinson's Poetry*. New Haven, CT, & London: Yale University Press, 1974.

Oberhaus, Dorothy R., *Emily Dickinson's Fascicles: Method & Meaning*. University Park, PA: Pennsylvania State University Press, 1995.

O'Keefe, Martha L., "This Edifice: Studies in the Structure of the (13) Fascicles of the poetry of Emily Dickinson". *Dickinson Studies*, Washington, DC, 42 (June 1982), 3–15.

Ollendorff, H. G., *New Method of Learniong to Read German*, 1846.

Orsini, Daniel J., "Emily Dickinson and the Romantic Use of Science". *Massachussetts Studies in English*, Amherst MA, 7–8, no. 41 (1981), 57–69.

Owen, Wilfred, *The Collected Poems of*, ed. by C. Day Lewis. London: Chatto and Windus, 1963.

Patterson, Rebecca, "Emily Dickinson's Debt to Günderode". *The Midwest Quarterly*, VIII (1967), 331–354.

Patterson, Rebecca, *Emily Dickinson's Imagery*. Amherst, MA: University of Massachusetts Press, 1979.

Plato, *Phaedo*.

Plato, *Symposium.*

Plato, *Timaeus.*

Pollak, Vivian R., *Dickinson: The Anxiety of Gender.* Ithaca, NY, & London: Cornell University Press, 1984.

Porter, David, *The Art of Emily Dickinson's Early Poetry.* Cambridge, MA: Harvard University Press, 1966.

Porter, David, *The Modern Idiom.* Cambridge, MA: Harvard University Press, 1981.

Richards, I. A., *Practical Criticsm.* London: Routledge and Kegan Paul [1929] 1976.

Ringler-Henderson, Ellin, "Poem 754". *Women's Studies,* New York, 16 (1989), nos. 1–2, 127–131.

Rollins, H. E. (ed.), *The Keats Circle: Letters and Papers 1816–1878.* Cambridge, MA: Harvard University Press, 1965.

Rosenbaum, S. P. (ed.), *A Concordance to the Poems of Emily Dickinson.* Ithaca, NY: Cornell University Press, 1964.

Rourke, C., *American Humor: A Study of The National Character,* Garden City, NY, 1931.

Rupp, R. (ed.), *Critics on Emily Dickinson* (John Crowe Ransom, David Porter, Albert Gelpi, Thomas H. Johnson, Archibald MacLeish, Susanne Wilson, et al.). Miami, FL: University of Miami Press, 1972.

Salska, A., "Emily Dickinson's Letters: The Making of a Poetics", in J. Maszewska (ed.), *Crossing Borders: American Literature and Other Artistic Media,* Lodz. Peoria, IL: Polish Scientific, Spoon River, 1992.

Schiller, F., *On the Aesthetic Education of Man in a Series of Letters,* ed. by Elizabeth M. Wilkinson & L. A. Willoughby. Oxford: Clarendon Press [1967] 1982.

Scholl, Diane G., "Emily Dickinson's Conversion Narratives: A Study of the Fascicles". *Studies in Puritan American Spirituality,* Lewiston, NY, 1 (1990), 170–201.

Sewall, Richard B., *The Life of Emily Dickinson.* New York: Farrar, Straus and Giroux, 1974.

Sewall, Richard B., *A Collection of Critical Essays.* Englewood Cliffs, NJ: Prentice-Hall, 1963.

Sewall, Richard B., *The Lyman Letters: New Light on Emily Dickinson and Her Family.* Amherst, MA: University of Massachusetts Press, 1965.

Sewall, Richard B., "Science and the Poet: Emily Dickinson's Herbarium and 'The Clue Divine'". *Harvard Library Bulletin*, Cambridge MA, 3, no. 1 (Spring 1992), 11–26.

Shakespeare, *Complete Works*, ed. by Peter Alexander. London & Glasgow: Collins [1951], 1966.

Shelley, P. B., *Shelley's Prose*, ed. by David Lee Clark. London: Fourth Estate, 1988.

Sherwood, William R., *Circumference and Circumstance: Stages in the Mind and Art of Emily Dickinson*. New York: Columbia University Press, 1968.

Shurr, William H. *New Poems of Emily Dickinson*. Chapel Hill, NC, & London: University of North Carolina Press, 1993.

Small, Judy Jo, *Positive as Sound: Emily Dickinson's Rhyme*. Athens, GA, & London: University of Georgia Press, 1990.

Spiller, Robert, *The Cycle of American Literature*. New York: Free Press, 1967.

Stephenson, R. H., *Goethe's Conception of Science and Knowledge*. Edinburgh: Edinburgh University Press, 1995.

Strich, Fritz, "Europe and the Romantic Movement". *German Life & Letters*, Oxford, II, no. 2 (January 1949), 85–90.

Tate, Allen, "Emily Dickinson", in *Saggi* (trans. as *On the Limits of Poetry*, 1948, and *The Forlorn Demon*, 1953). Rome: Edizioni di Storia e Letteratura, 1957, Ch. 8, 151–170 [see also: Denis Donoghue].

Thacrey, D. E., *Emily Dickinson's Approach to Poetry*. Lincoln, NE: University of Nebraska Press, 1954.

Thibault, Paul J., *Re-reading Saussure: The Dynamics of Signs in Social Life*. London: Routledge, 1997.

Thota, R. A., & Singh, S., *Emily Dickinson: The Metaphysical Tradition*. Atlantic Highlands, NJ: Humanities, 1982.

Tripp, R. P. "Spiritual Action in 'My Life had stood—a Loaded Gun'". *Papers on Language and Literature*, Edwardsville, 25, no. 3 (Summer 1989), 282–303.

Tselentis-Apostolidis, Persephone, "And I Will Be Socrates: Greek Elements in the Poetry of Dickinson". *Dickinson Studies*, Washington, DC, 52 (second half 1984), 3–21.

Van Wyck Brooks, *The Flowering of New England*. New York: Dutton & Co., 1932.

Waddell, Margot, & Harris Williams, Meg, *The Chamber of Maiden*

Thought: Literary Origins of the Psychoanalytic Model of the Mind. London: Routledge, 1991.

Waggoner, H., "The Transcendent Self". *Criticism: A Quarterly for Literature & the Arts*, Detroit, MI (1965), 297–334.

Wakoski, Diane, "Emily Dickinson and Robert Creeley: Maverick Writers of the Latin Lyric". *New Orleans Review*, New Orleans LA, 19, no. 1 (Spring 1992), 14–26.

Walsh, J. E., *The Hidden Life of Emily Dickinson*. New York: Simon and Schuster, 1971.

Ward, Theodora, *The Capsule of the Mind: Chapters in the Life of Emily Dickinson*. Cambridge, MA: The Belknap Press of Harvard University Press, 1961.

Watts, Isaac, *The Psalms, Hymns & Spiritual Songs*, ed. by S. Worcester. Boston, MA, 1819.

Weisbuch, Robert, *Emily Dickinson's Poetry*. Chicago, IL: University of Chicago Press, 1972.

White, Fred D., "'Sweet Skepticism of the Heart': Science in the Poetry of Emily Dickinson". *College Literature*, West Chester, PA, 19, no. 1 (February 1992), 121–128.

Wider, Sarah, "Corresponding Worlds: The Art of Emily Dickinson's Letters". *Emily Dickinson Journal*, 1 (1992), no. 1, 39–53.

Wilkinson, E. M., "Reflections after Translating Schiller's *Letters on the Aesthetic Education of Man*", in F. Norman (ed.), *Schiller: Bicentenary Lectures*. London, 1960, 46–82.

Willoughby, L. A., "'Name ist Schall und Rauch': On the Significance of Names for Goethe". *German Life & Letters*, Oxford, XVI, 3–4 (April & July 1963), 294–307.

Winters, Yvor, "Emily Dickinson and the Limits of Judgement", in *In Defense of Reason*. New York: William Morrow, 1947.

Winnington Ingram, R. P. "*Hippolytus*: A Study in Causation", Entretien sur l'Antiquité Classique, VI, *Euripide*, Fondation Hardt. Geneva: Vandoeuvres, 1960, 171–191.

Winnington Ingram, R. P. *Euripides and Dionysus*. Cambridge, UK: Cambridge University Press, 1948.

Wordsworth, William, *A Selection of his Finest Poems*, ed. by Stephen Gill & Duncan Wu. Oxford: Oxford University Press, 1995.

Wylder, Edith Perry Stamm, *The Last Face: Emily Dickinson's Manuscripts*. Albuquerque, NM: University of New Mexico Press, 1971.

INDEX

Index of names

Index of titles

Index of letters cited

Index of poems cited

Categories

This part of the index has been arranged into categories (A–G) that seemed most likely to be of use for reference in a study of this nature. There are in fact several item overlaps, especially between three major categories: between Category A, comprising networks of metaphor involving either imagery or apparently 'abstract' terms or both, Category B, comprising words or word-clusters that become fixed and really attain the status of concepts for ED, again, involving either abstract or more apparently 'image'-like terms or both (though I have never come across another poet in whose hands words have such incredible gymnastic fluidity, constantly, implicating every facet—sound-punning, etymology, visual-image, abstract–concrete interchanging etc., in addition to their immense drilling power), and between these the category of opposites (Category C). For these represent elements that constantly interacted with and re-created each other in Dickinson's method of working, I think something analogous to what E. M. Wilkinson began to describe as "interdependent variables" in her brilliantly discerning and powerfully eloquent essay on Schiller's aesthetic writings (*see*: "Reflections after Translating Schiller's *Letters on the Aesthetic Education of Man*", in *Schiller: Bicentenary Lectures*, ed. F. Norman, London, 1960, p. 81). So sometimes entries may appear in two categories, and often cross-reference is made to entries in another category; sometimes entries contain linked variants—or varying linkages—independently. In Category A I have tried to keep exclusively to her 'words' in the items and in the suggested examples of linkages that follow thus: (*see*: x; y; z); occasional gloss-interpretations are in square brackets. In Category B I have linked her item-'words' only to other sources in suggesting linkages, and not returned into her metaphorical networks, which can be sought in Category A. Other categories (D–G) are more 'external' to Dickinson's own work and for the most part stand happily alone. In the "traditional" category (E) I have, perhaps debatably, also included word-symbols from the (to her) very recent past, with the sole apology that she was quick to see them coming and stood on no ceremony in putting them to work. Finally, there is one area of distinction missing in this indexing of Dickinson's work, that one can begin to see enmeshed in the metaphor networks, but which I have been unable to pull out and put into focus, more than by suggestion, from the content of this study. Partly, I think, because I was at the outset lacking any solid grasp of usable concepts and terms for such phenomena myself. But partly, I also think, because it seems to me an area in experience that most deeply and cogently preoccupied and perplexed Dickinson herself—though she was fundamentally of a courageous and determinedly optimistic nature—and is, in practice, indeed still very mysterious to our understanding generally. And that is, the issue of what Schiller began to make distinct with his terms "honest and dishonest semblance", and the effective murder and life-giving intrinsic to these respective categories, which in turn was to become a cornerstone of Coleridge's concept of "living meaning", Dickinson's "the Alive". I mention it because it seems so very important an area in Dickinson's research to me now.

A. Networks of metaphor / concepts forming in ED

B. Concepts formed, becoming fixed, in ED

C. Groups of opposites

D. Other concepts, applied to her work/in line with hers

E. Traditional symbols, forms, concepts

F. Structure–syntax–mode

G. Other—factual/historical information/literal links